THE FEMALE SUFFERING BODY

Gender, Culture, and Politics in the Middle East
miriam cooke, Simona Sharoni, *and* Suad Joseph

Other titles in Gender, Culture, and Politics in the Middle East

Arab and Arab American Feminisms: Gender, Violence, and Belonging
Rabab Abdulhadi, Evelyn Alsultany, and Nadine Naber, eds.

Contesting Realities: The Public Sphere and Morality in Southern Yemen
Susanne Dahlgren

Embracing the Divine: Passion and Politics in the Christian Middle East
Akram Fouad Khater

Ideal Refugees: Gender, Islam, and the Sahrawi Politics of Survival
Elena Fiddian Qasmiyeh

Masculine Identity in the Fiction of the Arab East since 1967
Samira Aghacy

"Off the Straight Path": Illicit Sex, Law, and Community in Ottoman Aleppo
Elyse Semerdjian

Pioneers or Pawns? Women Health Workers and the Politics of Development in Yemen
Marina de Regt

Words, Not Swords: Iranian Women Writers and the Freedom of Movement
Farzaneh Milani

THE FEMALE SUFFERING BODY

Illness and Disability in Modern Arabic Literature

ABIR HAMDAR

Syracuse University Press

First Edition 2014
14 15 16 17 18 19 6 5 4 3 2 1

∞ The paper used in this publication meets the minimum requirements of the American National Standard for Information Sciences—Permanence of Paper for Printed Library Materials, ANSI Z39.48-1992.

For a listing of books published and distributed by Syracuse University Press, visit www.SyracuseUniversityPress.syr.edu.

ISBN: 978-0-8156-3365-5 (cloth) 978-0-8156-5290-8 (e-book)

Library of Congress Control Number: 2014955102

Manufactured in the United States of America

To my family,
my husband Arthur,
and my daughter Aya.

Abir Hamdar is a lecturer in Arabic in the School of Modern Languages and Cultures at Durham University, UK.

CONTENTS

ACKNOWLEDGMENTS

I would like to thank the many friends and colleagues who have helped me in all sorts of ways during the process of researching and writing *The Female Suffering Body.*

Firstly, this book began life as a PhD thesis written under the supervision of Professor Sabry Hafez at the School of Oriental and African Studies, University of London. I am very grateful to the Felix Scholars whose generous award of a scholarship made my studies possible. I must also thank Professor Hafez for his invaluable support and unrivaled knowledge of Arabic literature and culture. My thanks must also go to the external examiner of my thesis, Professor Hoda Elsadda, for her enthusiasm for the project and her subsequent support in my career.

I would particularly like to thank my parents-in-law Anne and John Bradley, Hilary Hinds, and Jackie Stacey for all their support. My gratitude also goes to: Lina Abiad, Robert and Marion Appelbaum, Marie-Claire Barnet, Mayra and Rami Beydoun, Sally Bushell, Shirley Chew, Rachid al-Daif, Michael Dillon, Ziad Elmarsafy, Zahera Harb, Sawsan Maktabi, Marianne Marroum, Nayanika Mookherjee, Lindsey Moore, Dalia Mostafa, Shuruq Naguib, Liz Oakley-Brown, Ken Seigneurie, Paul and Janet Starkey, Edward Welch, Thomas Wynn, and Anastasia Valassopoulos. I would also like to thank my colleagues in the Arabic Department at Durham University.

At Syracuse University Press, I am greatly indebted to editor-in-chief Suzanne E. Guiod, the general editors of the Gender, Culture, and Politics in the Middle East series as well as the anonymous readers of my manuscript. They all contributed to making this a much better book than it would otherwise have been. I would also like to give special thanks to

Afaf Zurayk for giving me permission to use one of her wonderful artworks for the book cover.

Finally, I would like to thank my parents—Salwa and Hussein Hamdar—and my siblings for endless amounts of love and support. Also, a million thanks to Arthur for being the most wonderful and caring husband: This book would never have been possible without you.

And to our precious daughter, Aya: *inti noor albi*.

AUTHOR NOTE

In order to make this book more accessible to the Anglophone reader, I adopt a general system of transliteration and use only the *ayn* and *hamza*.

I also present names and titles of people, places, and texts in the form most familiar to an English-speaking audience and/or the form used by the works under discussion themselves.

I refer primarily to English translations of the Arabic texts, where they are available. In the absence of an existing English translation at the time of writing, translations from the Arabic are my own.

Finally, a section of chapter 2 was published as "Female Physical Illness and Disability in Arab Women's Writing" in *Feminist Theory* 11.2 (2010) and a section of chapter 3 was published as "Aesthetic Visibility: Female Illness/Disability in Hasan Dawud's *Makyaj Khafif*" in *al-Abhath: Journal of the Centre of Arab and Middle Eastern Studies* 58–59 (2010–2011).

The Female Suffering Body

INTRODUCTION

In the closing pages of one of the most famous Arabic novels in history, a woman falls ill and dies. It is not the first time illness or death has afflicted a character in the course of the novel. As its readers already know, the woman's son has been violently killed years earlier during a nationalist demonstration, her son-in-law and grandchildren have also suffered premature death from disease, and her once-virile and patriarchal husband endures years of suffering and ill health before his own sudden death from a heart attack. Yet, there is a key difference with the depiction of the illness of this woman because, quite simply, it is not depicted at all. To be sure, we learn a little of the woman's illness through the testimony of her sons, but—in stark contrast to the case of her husband and dead son—the reader is not permitted entry into the room of the sick woman, let alone into her dying consciousness. The third-person omniscient narrator does not even disclose the nature of the illness that kills her. Perhaps most interestingly of all, the novel does not end with her death but merely with the anticipation of it: the famous concluding scene describes two of her sons walking back to the family home in Cairo to await the inevitable end. In *al-Sukkariya* (Sugar Street, 1957) by Naguib Mahfouz—for, of course, this is the book I am talking about—the figure of Amina is quite literally *hors-texte*, outside of the text, a singular literary and aesthetic absence at the heart of arguably the defining Arabic novel.

It is the story of this absence, and of what comes to fill it, that the present book aims to tell. As I will seek to show in what follows, Mahfouz's exclusion of Amina from *al-Thulathiyya* (The Cairo Trilogy, 1956–1957) is merely a symptom of a much larger abjection of the physically sick and disabled female body in Arabic literature more generally. To appreciate the extent to which the sick female body still remains largely outside the Arab literary imaginary, it is only necessary to recall the rich, complex, and variegated representations of female illness in Western literature over the last two centuries: Where, for example, are the Arab equivalents to Jane Austen's *Persuasion* (1818), to Charlotte Perkins Gilman's *The Yellow Wallpaper* (1892), Henry James's *The Wings of The Dove* (1902), Margaret Atwood's *Bodily Harm* (1981), and Jeanette Winterson's *Written on the Body* (1992)? If the representation of gender and illness in European and North American literature has spawned an entire critical industry—including the now burgeoning field of the Medical Humanities—it is also striking that to date, few, if any, studies have appeared that address the field of Arabic literature. In the early years of the twenty-first century, it seems that Arabic literary criticism still awaits its own Michel Foucault, Susan Sontag, Elaine Scarry, Byron J. Good, or Arthur Kleinman.

To be fair, Arabic literary and cultural criticism—like its Western equivalent—has extensively mined the field of "the body" as a social, cultural, and political signifier over the last few decades. Nevertheless, such studies have by and large focused on the representation of the body in general, and the female sexual body in particular, rather than the impaired and ill body.[1] Perhaps most problematically, Arabic corporeal criticism arguably remains trapped in an excessively linguistic or constructionist paradigm which automatically tends to depict the body as little more than a metaphor for some prior linguistic, social, or political body—most obviously the body politic of the nation. In this respect, Arabic criticism has not undergone the affective turn that has been so prominent in Western literary and cultural criticism over the last few years: the body as a feeling

1. See Ibrahim Mahmoud (2002) for a historical reading of the sexuality of both male and female bodies in Arabic literature and culture. For a study of the representation of the body in Arabic literature see Sa'id al-Wakil (2004). For studies on the symbolism and representation of female sexual bodies in Arabic literature and culture see, for example, Fedwa Malti-Douglas (1991); *Sexuality and Arab Women* (2002/2003); Evelyne Accad (1990); Therese Saliba (1996).

and suffering somatic entity—rather than a social or cultural construct—still remains a largely undiscovered country.[2]

Why does Arabic literature cast a veil of silence—if I may be permitted to use such a fraught metaphor—over female physical illness and disability? How have Arab writers obscured the body of the sick woman? And what might enable us to bring that body back out into the open? To even attempt to tell the story of female physical illness and disability in the Arabic novel, the critic is confronted with the problem of how to reckon with its (highly) conspicuous absence. Firstly, we should note that the numbers of modern prose texts in Arabic that depict the female suffering body are meager. Even when the Arabic novel and short story does represent female illness and disability, they remain spectral, barely visible presences at the margin of the text. For Mahfouz, just as for the Arabic novel and short story more generally, it is almost as if female subjectivity and female illness/disability are incompatible with each other: Amina effectively disappears from *The Cairo Trilogy*—a text in which she has arguably been the central character—the moment she succumbs to illness. If the story of the sick female body in Arabic literature is largely the story of an absence (an absence that persists even when the character is present), we will also see that there are some causes for optimism in contemporary fiction. The last few years have witnessed the emergence of a number of works that begin to fill in the gap where female physical illness and disability should always have been. In spite of such promising developments, though, it is clear that the task of textually recuperating the sick female body—of bringing it back to the center of the narrative, of allowing

2. Fedwa Malti-Douglas's *Blindness and Autobiography: Al-Ayyam of Taha Husayn* (1988) is one of the few books to deconstruct Egyptian Taha Husayn's experience of blindness as it is narrated in his autobiography and to perceive it as both a physical and social condition. However, in her book *Woman's Body, Woman's Word: Gender and Discourse in Arabo-Islamic Writing* (1991), Malti-Douglas devotes a chapter to establishing parallels between Husayn's physical blindness in real life and its ramifications as they have been depicted in his *al-Ayyam* and the feminine, sighted, but "devalued body" in Nawal al-Saadawi's novel *Mudhakkirat Tabiba* (111–29).

it to speak for itself in its own voice without subjecting it to external social, cultural, and political discourses—has only just begun.

This book will examine the representation of female physical illness and disability in selected novels and short stories by Arab male and female writers of the Levant and Egypt from the period of 1950 to the present. It will focus on the various ways that sick and disabled female characters have been depicted in these works, the roles allotted to them within the space of the narrative, as well as the symbolic meaning their presence or absence is intended to signify. At the same time, the study will also interrogate the larger social, religious, and political discourses that have scripted female physical sickness within the Arab world. To quickly sketch my overall objective, what follows will bring together literary criticism with sociology and anthropology of health and illness to offer a critical genealogy of the sick female body in Arabic literature—where it comes from, how it has been repressed, and where it is becoming visible today. Perhaps more precisely, it will seek to answer the following crucial questions: What exactly constitutes "female illness and disability" in Arabic literature? How is it represented differently by writers of different genders, periods, and countries? How have Arab writers sought to represent or repress the female body in pain? How can we read female illness and disability in the Arab world? Is it possible to understand it as more than a discursive construct, a symbol of social and political ideologies? Is the new generation of writers constructing new modes of narrative to speak of female physical illness and disability? To what extent is contemporary Arabic literature now combating the prevailing discourse of female sickness and re-imagining what it means to be a sick woman?

Illness, Sickness, and Disability

In order to even begin to address these questions, however, we need to clarify some of the core terms that will appear again and again throughout this study: illness, sickness, and disability. It is no exaggeration to say that one of the central preoccupations of any discussion of health and illness is now a semantic one: what precisely do we mean by such terms as illness, sickness, malaise, and physical impairment? To the casual observer, the vast array of medical, social, and philosophical interpretations of illness now available means that the term seems to "lose itself in the maze of disciplines, of cultures and of history" (Augé & Herzlich 1995, 1). Yet the starting premise of all such definitions of illness is inevitably the idea of what constitutes health. For the World Health Organization (to borrow the most-cited definition) health is "a state of complete physical, mental and social well being, not merely the absence of disease or infirmity" (WHO 1990; Hardey 1998). If this definition has been widely and officially adopted, some critics have criticized its underlying idealism: it seems to assume an impossible totality of "body, mind and soul realized in the Golden Ages but long since forfeited" (Seedhouse 1986; Lewis 1953, 110). Nevertheless, the WHO definition has also been praised for encompassing "social, psychological and subjective dimensions" as well as purely clinical factors and it has also attracted support from various lay perspectives (Hardey 1998, 28). In one of the first studies to interview participants regarding their view of health and illness, for instance, Claudine Herzlich defines health not only as the absence of illness but places a great emphasis on positive feelings about oneself and on social relations in general as well as the ability of the body to thwart illness (1973).

It is perhaps with Leon Eisenberg's early efforts to differentiate between the various signifiers of health and illness that we encounter a greater specificity of meaning. To quickly summarize his argument, Eisenberg contends that "patients suffer 'illnesses'; physicians diagnose and treat 'disease'. . . . Illnesses are experiences of disvalued changes in states of being and social function; diseases are abnormalities in the structure and function of body organs and systems" (1977, 22). Firstly, then, disease becomes an "objective or thing-like quality" and involves a dysfunction in the "biological, physiological or chemical processes of the body" (Hardey 1998, 29). According to this definition, disease is what Arthur Kleinman calls a "problem from the practitioner's perspective" and is "reconfigured only as an alteration in biological structure or functioning" (1988, 5–6). Yet as Byron J. Good notes, "disease is located in the body as a physical object or physiological state," while the "body is subject, the very grounds of subjectivity or experiences in the world." By this reckoning, "the diseased body is not simply the object of cognition and knowledge, or representation in mental states and the works of medical sciences. It is at the same time a disordered agent of experience" (1994, 116). This turns illness from an objective medical condition into the *experience* of disease, which is grounded in the subjective feelings of the body.

Despite, or because of, these suggestive distinctions, the term "illness" continues to take on different meanings in different disciplinary contexts: it remains "polysemic or multivocal," bespeaking of multiple meanings. It is not enough to locate it on the personal or subjective level of the individual's experience of his or her own body because the subjective is always inter-subjective, always opening up to and negotiating with the lives and bodies of others (Kleinman 1988, 8–9). Accordingly, the meaning of illness is affected by cultural determinants that influence "perception, labelling and explanations, and valuation of the discomforting experience" (Kleinman, Eisenberg, and Good 2006, 141; 1978). For Herzlich and Pierret, "we cannot think of [illness], or its meaning, without at the same time thinking about the world and society" (1985, 145–51). If illness exists in space, it also exists in time: Good writes that "illness is grounded in human historicity, in the temporality of individuals and families and communities," adding that "illness cannot be represented all at once or from a single vantage. It is constituted, rather, as a 'network of perspectives'" (1994, 157–58). Perhaps it is here—at the point of chiasmus where the individual body meets the social body—that the possibility of what Susan Sontag famously calls illness as metaphor arises (1990). On the one hand, the ill individual internalizes a set of social, political, and ideological discourses about what his or her illness means: he or she may begin to feel socially useless or politically impotent. On the other, the ill individual also projects outward from the illness a "truth" about the order of the world itself: the sick body reflects a sick or corrupted society (Kleinman 1988). In its endless traffic back and forth between the individual and his or her environment, the concept of illness mutates once again to become a new term: sickness.

To Howard Brody, it is "sickness" which captures the inescapably social dimension to the lived experience of illness. According to Brody, various signs coalesce in the idea of the sick body including (1) an experience of a certain disturbance of both body and self and a disorder in one's "personhood"; (2) a sense of abnormality brought about through a comparison with a "reference class"; (3) a reality that changes one's social function and relations in a manner that is shaped by cultural values; and (4) a condition that alters the "hierarchy of natural systems" such as the biological, psychological, and social systems of which one is part (2003, 44).[3] In short, sickness obtains its definition from the relationships it holds with society and social systems at large: one is never, as it were, sick alone.

If illness temporarily disrupts one's ability to perform social functions, it is disability that could render that interruption permanent or life-long. To David T. Mitchell and Sharon L. Snyder, illness always holds the promise of an end—be it through treatment or death—whereas disability is often seen as a chronic state where treatment or cure cannot be offered. They argue that disability "bears the onus of a permanent biological condition" and disabled persons "do not enjoy the biological luxury of recovery that informs the more transient experience of illness, disease, or disorder" (2004, 3). By the same token, Julia Epstein argues that "whatever their cause, diseases remain *processes* that follow a *course* . . . [while] disability is the absence of ability" (1995, 11). For Mitchell and Snyder, disease is seen as "follow[ing] a *course*," and this helps to domesticate it "by virtue of a belief in [its] determinant status," whereas disability surpasses "a culture's predictive capacities and effective interventions" (2004, 3). This essential lack or surplus of determined meaning is one of the reasons why defining disability and disabled persons becomes such a fraught exercise.

Perhaps the shifting meaning of the term "disability" itself bears witness to this essential problem of definition. According to the World Health Organization's early definition, disability is "any loss or abnormality of psychological/physiological or anatomical structure or function" (1980, 27). Even though one can metaphorically describe such phenomena as poverty as a form of social disability, its pervasive meaning is a "biopsychological one," and its classical forms are "blindness, lameness, mental deficiency [and] chronic incapacitating illness" (Ingstad and Whyte 1995, 3). Yet, the

3. Brody also notes that each one of these distinctions "could be misused" but they are helpful in that they enhance the understanding of the experiences and narrative accounts of sickness itself (2003, 44).

definition of disability as an impairment in the operation of the body or mind echoes Kleinman's definition of disease itself as a "malfunctioning of biological and/or psychological processes" (1980, 72). To many contemporary critics, the basic biological/medical definition of disability still inevitably bleeds into a social one when the malfunctioning of biological processes comes to be experienced phenomenologically, psychologically, and emotionally. Quite simply, disability—like disease—creates a harrowing world where "problems about personhood, responsibility and the meaning of differences" surface (Ingstad and Whyte 1995, 4). By bringing about an "altered sense of selfhood, one that has been savaged by the partial destruction of the body," disability ceases to be merely a physical concern and becomes an "ontology, a condition of . . . being in the world" (Murphy 1990, 90). For contemporary critics working in disability studies, like Lennard J. Davis, the whole concept of disability is thus an "extraordinarily unstable one" that "expands and contracts to include 'normal' people as well" (1995, xv). Such arguments are echoed by Clare Barker: "[D]isabilities differ drastically in form and function and may be permanent, temporary, stable, progressive, chronic, episodic, medicated, or 'cured', the disabled constituency of a population is always in flux" (2011, 17). The evolving nature of the concept of disability and its complex categorization can now be noted in the new definition adopted by the WHO in 2011, and reviewed in 2013, which sees disability as a combination of biological, social, and individual factors, stating on their website that "disability is the interaction between individuals with a health condition . . . and personal and environmental factors." This classification perceives disability as more than a biological or medical impairment and acknowledges that disability involves physical limitations at the same time as it is experienced socially and subjectively. In short, "disability infuses every aspect of [the disabled person's] social being" (Mitchell and Snyder 2004, 3).

What will the terms "disease," "illness," and "sickness" mean in the context of this study? To be sure, I will not neglect the biological meaning and material significance of such terms and I am particularly wary of (inevitable but deeply problematic) attempts to transform a biological condition/limitation into a mere social or cultural metaphor. It is, however, not possible to discuss the female suffering body—and particularly the fictional body—without also confronting the subjective and social dimensions of its infliction: disease, illness, and sickness cross-contaminate one another. Accordingly, a female character who suffers from tuberculosis or breast cancer, for example, cannot simply be seen as the subject of a medical disease because we must also consider the lived, social, and cultural experience of that disease. Firstly, then, it is essential to explore how the female character experiences her own disease, how that disease is perceived by the members of her society, how it impacts upon her personal and social sense of identity, and how it is narrativized by the text itself. If we are to do justice to the multiple dimensions of disease, we need to track how disease "metastasizes" beyond the medical sphere, so to speak, to become illness and sickness. In Good's powerful formulation: "Disease occurs not only in the body—in the sense of an ontological order in the great chain of being—but in time, in place, in history, and in the context of lived experience and the social world. Its effect is on the body in the world!" (1994, 133).

For the purposes of this study, however, we must also reckon with the fact that disease occurs in a very singular world indeed: the work of literature. It will quickly become clear that the definitions of illness and disability advanced by the discourse of Arabic literature are often very different from the ones offered by contemporary health discourse. As we will see, terms like "illness," "sickness," and "disability" sometimes leak into one another, sometimes are deployed interchangeably, and sometimes are not used at all. My aim of addressing the representation of female physical illness and disability in one single book stems from this very fact: disease, illness, and disability are frequently collapsed together in Arabic literature. If at times I am guilty of describing very different experiences such as cancer, blindness, infertility, and physical impairment as if they were comparable or equivalent in the discussions that follow, then, I should stress that I only do so because the discourse of illness and disability in the Middle East, and in the Arab world specifically, conflates these experiences. In other words, I am all too aware that cancer, blindness, and infertility are different, but, as my textual analysis will highlight, they are not treated as such in the narratives under discussion. They are all seen as examples of a general unarticulated "problem" or "disorder" with women.

This is why we need to add one final term to the lexicon of health, illness, sickness, and disability we have been developing in this Introduction: "malaise." According to Clouser, Culver, and Gert, "A person has a malady if and only if he or she has a condition, other than a rational belief or desire, such that he or she is suffering, or at increased risk of suffering an evil (death, pain, disability, loss of freedom or opportunity or loss of pleasure) in the absence of a distinct sustaining cause" (1981, 36). To be clear about my own use of this term, "malaise" does not entail any biological malfunction (and could even include conditions such as menopause and menstruation), but I will deploy it to describe characters whose experience of illness and physical impairment is not only characterized by loss of freedom or pleasure but is further attached to irrational myths of evil and shame. Perhaps the fact that the term "malady" is generally employed in reference to what Brody dubs "asymptomatic" conditions (2003, 62 n5) makes it particularly apposite in the case of Arabic literature because many of the suffering women we will encounter in this book are occluded to the point where the precise symptoms and nature of their illness is never disclosed: disease, sickness, and illness are transformed into a shadowy, asymptomatic malady by a narrative gaze that is always directed elsewhere. In Mahfouz's *Sugar Street*, for example, Amina is never symptomatically sick, ill, or diseased. She dies, strictly speaking, from a malaise.

Finally, my title—*The Female Suffering Body*—should be read in the same discursive context. My intention is not to naturalize illness and disability nor to imply that women who are ill and disabled are necessarily "suffering" women. As we will see, my argument is rather that the subject position of "suffering" is imposed upon the women of Arabic literature from without by the prevailing discourses. In what follows, I seek to tell the story of how women are able to resist these symbolic discourses and start to narrate their own bodies.

Female Illness and Disability in Arabic Literature and Culture

In order to fine-tune the theoretical framework I will be using a little more, I now want to turn to the meaning of health and illness in Arabic literature and culture. It is every bit as problematic to define health and illness in Arabic culture as it is in the West, albeit for the diametrically opposite reason: whereas the West arguably suffers from too many definitions of health, the Arab world has very few. As Hania Sholkamy posits: "Describing social processes through the lens of embodied experiences and conditions is an undervalued tool of social analysis" (2004, 112). For Soheir Morsy, as well, Arab intellectual discourse suffers from an acute lack of studies that specifically concern the connection between gender and health. There is a dire need to acknowledge women's health as a wing of past social relations that involve national formation, undeveloped social class and masculine hegemony (Basyouny 1998, 50). If any such studies exist, they generally belong to the field of medical anthropology and are concerned with how "the idioms of Islam, humeral medicine, or spirit possession" foreground medical performances and values (Sholkamy 2004, 112). Others explore the history of the medical establishment and take into account gendered discourses and practices that shaped the development of medicine and health care in the region, especially Egypt.[4]

It is also unfortunate that the vast majority of the available studies focus on understanding attitudes to health in one country only rather than on providing an overview of the complexities at play within the wider region. Accordingly, Egypt[5] and Iraq—after the sanctions—seem to have ignited more investigation than, say, Lebanon or Syria. Similarly, most of the studies that center on the correlation between health discourses and gender relations expose problems such as mental health, infertility, family planning, reproductive health, and lately weight issues.[6] By contrast, discussion of the physically impaired and ill body, the meanings found

4. See, for example, Hibba Abugideiri (2010); Khaled Fahmy (1998); Mervat F. Hatem (1997); LaVerne Kuhnke (1974).

5. This, according to Cynthia Nelson, is due to the fact that Egypt is both a "contemporary society" and one seeped in its "ancient root." Its "highly westernized institutions exist simultaneously with traditional practices and services" such as midwives and religious healers and, thus, makes it a fertile ground for medical anthropological studies (1977, 19–22).

6. See Evelyn Early (1993); Marcia C. Inhorn (1994); Mohammed T. Abou Saleh, Yahia Younis, and Lina Karim (1998).

in personal testimonies and narratives about this body, and the social and cultural realities these narratives expose, are generally absent.

To turn to the many studies of the relationship between Islam and health, we find a number of prevalent foci. Firstly, many studies seek to show how the Islamic emphasis on patience, resignation, and acceptance produces passive patients. It is also possible to observe another strand that focuses on devotional practices that rely on scriptures of the written word and on "prophetic medicine" such as the use of cupping (Hijama)—which is gaining more public support in nations like Egypt. Yet another focus is upon the Islamic prohibition on family planning and control (Sholkamy 2004, 113–15). Perhaps more intriguingly, a large number of medical anthropological studies of illness in the Arab world, especially earlier ones, have focused on humeral medicine—a practice that places importance on balance and equilibrium in attaining well-being. In Arabic culture, humeral medicine not only emphasizes moderation in food but also emotions: excessive emotional states such as jealousy, yearning, and fear are also major determinants of health (Early 1988, 65–83).

One particularly intriguing question in the study of the relation between Islam and health—particularly from the perspective of women—is the function of religious pilgrimages and the veneration of saints in patients' experience of illness, and their search for healing and salvation. As a number of studies have shown, such religious practices are heavily gendered in nature: they are largely performed by women, whereas men are either embarrassed by, or feel contempt for them (Mernissi 1977; Tapper 1990; Inhorn 1994). For many women in the Middle East and the Arab world, then, the experience of illness and the search for healing involves visiting holy shrines and praying to saints to intercede on their behalf. In Marcia C. Inhorn's words, the "belief in *baraka* and the abilities of *baraka*-bestowing dead *shuyukh* to perform miraculous cures . . . brings hope to those whose health problems seem intractable or who have failed to find relief in other therapeutic venues" (1994, 220).[7]

7. As Inhorn notes, it is crucial to draw a distinction between *munagimin* and "blessed *shaikhs*." The latter, she explains, are "typically (but not necessarily) founders or followers"

More widely, the question of the relationship between Islam and health has also produced a new body of scholarly literature related to Islam and bioethics, in the context of the wider Middle East and the Arab world. This body of literature raises complex and multifaceted issues and highlights the relationship between religion and science by focusing on the position of Islamic religious authorities toward technical and medical advancements such as the use of in-vitro fertilization, donor gametes, and surrogacy. They also address the burgeoning of *fatwas* (religious proclamations), which attempt to clarify Islam's position toward these advancements, particularly in relation to reproductive health, and even investigate whether it is permissible for Muslims to seek such procedures (Lane and Rubinstein 1991; Zuhur 1992). In still another area, studies on the relationship between Islam and medical technologies also focus on the differing opinions between both Sunni and Shi'ite religious authorities regarding biotechnological procedures (Inhorn 2003; Clarke 2006).

For many socio-medical anthropologists in the Arab world, one of the most controversial focal points of research on health and illness has been the phenomenon of "spirit possession" and, especially, the instrumental role it plays in diagnosing illness and curing it through such acts as exorcism. It is perhaps here (even more strongly than in the case of Islam) that the gender dynamics of health and illness come into play and, particularly, in the distribution of power between subject and clinician. According to Evelyn Early, for example, spirit possession is a means through which women evade confinement (1988, 65–83). To put it in Heba el-Kholy's words, spirit possession is "a language of protest" that establishes and redefines the perimeters of social relationships by enabling women who share the same predicament to meet within a female-dominated space and enact certain ceremonies to drive spirits away. This facilitates the establishment of a form of kinship among the women and provides them with a "culturally legitimate and honorable way to communicate 'immodest' sentiments" (2004, 21–29). In Cynthia Nelson's account, spirit possession is

of Sufi orders whose presence and history in Egypt goes as far back as the tenth century (1994, 109).

an expression of idioms of somatic states that are culturally integral to the Middle East (1971, 194–209), and the majority of ethnographic studies from Egypt, Morocco, and Tunisia seem to confirm a close correlation between spirit possession and reproductive problems.[8]

If earlier research in the field places great stress on spirit possession as a diagnostic tool for illness in Arab cultures, more recent work has called this relation into question. To Inhorn, who has written one of the most compelling anthropological studies on reproduction and reproductive technologies in the context of the Arab world (especially Egypt), it is undoubtedly true that some women espouse spirit possession "as a socially acceptable 'sick role'" when no explanation or cure is provided for their predicament (1994, 200) but she goes on to argue that spirit possession remains "overdetermined as a cause of affliction" particularly in relation to infertility. In her fieldwork on infertility among poor, urban Egyptian women, Inhorn notes that possession rarely figured in infertile women's "lived experience" nor in their management of the problem and their search for conception (1994, 201). Perhaps more importantly, Inhorn's interviewees often ridiculed the notion that their infertility might be caused by spirit possession, asserting that it is all "nonsense and a product of the imagination." Even those women who accepted the idea of spirit beings often spoke of this in terms of their "*qarina*" or spirit-sister, "a spirit-counterpart, who lives underground" and who is believed to be a "'twin' or a woman's 'reflection.'" The twin sister is akin to an angel who has the interests of "her earthly sister at heart" (1994, 196–97). These spirit-counterparts are seen as harmless and if angered can be appeased through animal sacrifice or by providing milk, sweets, or scented soaps and essences (204). For Inhorn's interviewees, it is also striking that spirit possession was often dismissed as a delusion brought about by the weakened physical and mental state of the ill woman: she is someone who "can't move and just sleeps on the ground and she's not herself mentally" (quoted in Inhorn 1994, 200).

8. See, for example, Laila el-Hamamsy (1972); Soheir Morsy (1978, 1993); Marielouise Creyghton (1977).

For the majority of ethnographers and anthropologists—regardless of their position on the reality of the connection between spirit possession and clinical illness—the fact remains that spirit possession is a means of female empowerment. It is possible to make the same claim about Arab discourses on fertility: they arm women with a measure of agency by stressing their role in the making and producing of families (Faour 1989, 254–63).[9] As Early sums it up, fertility allows women to take the upper hand within families and communities by granting women the power to "withhold [reproduction] through birth control" and thus to unsettle the man's need for a family. It is equally clear that a capacity to bear many children can bestow additional rights for women from their husbands while also making divorce more difficult and restricting the husband's financial means to marry another wife (1993, 103). However, if female identity becomes tied to fertility, then a woman's health also becomes intimately connected to that of her children: "A wife and mother bears ultimate responsibility for producing a family and keeping them healthy," Early argues, and "she is deficient in her role if she does not exert effort to produce and cure children" (1993, 104). The measure of agency that fertility accords is, thus, imperilled. In this respect, a woman's health becomes a microcosm of her children's health rather than of her own subjectivity.

Just as discourses on health and illness in the Arab region have perceived fertility as a means toward the empowerment of women within a patriarchal system, so they also argue that fertility allows women to become active participants in the political struggle of the nation. Take the case of Palestine, for example, where women's reproductive health is seen as crucial in the national political fight. To conceive, particularly sons, is to become "the mothers of the nation" (Fargues 2000, 469). The fertility of the woman becomes a prerequisite and an affirmation of the fertility of the nation (Fargues 2000, 464–65). This relationship between nationalist and reproductive discourses is perhaps most extensively explored in Rhoda Ann Kanaaneh's ethnographic study *Birthing the Nation: Strategies*

9. For a comprehensive study of women and reproductive health in Egypt see, for example, Hind Khattab, Nabil Younis, and Huda Zurak (2000).

of Palestinian Women in Israel (2002). For Kanaaneh, women's bodies become the site of nationalist agendas whereby they are expected to reproduce more citizens to sustain the survival of the people and as part of a "demographic war" between both sides. In a kind of biopolitical equivalent to an arms race, Kanaaneh's study reveals the ways in which Israeli discourses on the nation-state employ the notion of the Arab demographic threat and high Palestinian fertility to urge Israeli women to be as fertile (2002).

This emphasis on women's health in relation to their reproductive capacity is arguably symptomatic of what Inhorn has described as "the reproductive essentialization of women's lives" (2006, 350). In her review of ethnographic studies on women's health both in Western and non-Western cultures (including the Arab world), Inhorn argues that while one could make the case that the "overwhelming focus on women and their reproduction is empowering—given the centrality of reproduction in women's lives and its function as a fundamental source of women's power in many societies around the globe—essentializing characterizations of women that continue to tie them to the realm of reproduction are both unfortunate and potentially constraining" (2006, 350). Perhaps we might say that the role of "mother of the nation" is bought by denying women any other role than mother.

Finally, the last few years have also witnessed the emergence of studies that interrogate the relationship between health and economy and, in particular, the extent to which an individual's economic status determines their sense of well-being. To take just one example, Montasser M. Kamal argues that the ways in which (Arab and more specifically Egyptian) patients present their illness and body to their physician is predetermined by the patient's awareness of his/her socio-economic position. It is contended that patients who come from middle class backgrounds will make sure they dress well before heading to a private clinic in order to affirm their socio-economic superiority. At the same time, Montasser cites the example of how female patients will use foreign words (English or French) to describe their symptoms so as to assert their own social and cultural capital. However, what is most revealing about Montasser's study is that it also emphasizes gender anxieties at the heart of one's perception of his/her illness. For Montasser, female patients habitually resort to silence about their illness because they worry that their body will become a contested space within their family. Specifically, one female patient called Amina avoids telling her husband and mother of her fertility problems because she believes that her husband will think she does not wish to become pregnant while her mother will blame her husband for attempting to turn her body into a mere reproductive organ. In a similar vein, Amina cannot divulge her illness concerns to her work colleagues because they do not come from the same socio-economic milieu. They are "baladi, coming from humble standards" and hence cannot possibly fathom what she is experiencing (2004, 65–90).

What, to conclude this brief *tour d'horizon*, is missing from Arab discourses on health and illness, especially when compared to their Western equivalents? It could be argued that it is precisely the social and cultural dimensions where disease becomes illness and illness becomes sickness. Unfortunately, Arab studies on chronic illness, disability, and other physical ailments have mainly provided statistical data and medical findings rather than targeted fully the social and cultural scope of these and other illness.[10] To refer to the example of Iraq, it is striking that research has repeatedly dealt with the impact of the sanctions and the use of uranium on the health of the population, but has so far failed to tackle the social repercussions these problems have had on individual and collective Iraqi selves. Even though the dismal conditions of Iraqi women have become the subject of much scrutiny, the result tends to be a largely quantitative comparison of mortality rates between mothers and their children.[11] In this respect, we see that a woman's health is repeatedly explored as a signifier of the health of her family and other subjects, rather than of her own.

Secondly, studies of Lebanon and Syria have tied women's health to notions of family planning and, more importantly, to the idea that a woman's well-being is at risk because she remains a passive victim of

10. An exception is Ruqayya Zeilani and Jane E. Seymour's study of real narratives told by women in intensive care in Jordan (2010).

11. See, for example, Rania Masri (2003); Richard Garfield and Beth Osborne Daponte (2000); Nadje al-Ali (2000).

patriarchal standards. In one of the earliest articles to address women and AIDS in Lebanon, the focus is not on the lived experience of the women victims themselves but rather on the high risk of contracting this autoimmune condition from one's husband. The article points out that women's acquiescence to their husband's desire not to use a condom during sexual intercourse exposes them to a greater risk of becoming infected. In this sense, it is male control over female sexuality that becomes the decisive factor in the spread of the AIDS epidemic among the female population (Abul-Husn 1994, 14–16).[12]

Perhaps more surprisingly still, very little work has focused on the harrowing experience of cancer among Arab women. It is true that studies have revealed an explosion in the number of female cancer patients in the Arab world, but the social experience of this illness itself has almost been obliterated. Arguably, the only exception is Fedwa Malti-Douglas's excellent contribution to this subject in her book *Medicines of the Soul: Female Bodies and Sacred Geographies in a Transnational Islam* which considers how illnesses like AIDS and breast cancer "play across religion" and in the context of the Arab/Muslim world (2001, xviii). Even as the Western world has seen the publication of numerous autobiographical narratives that transmit the experiences of women with cancer,[13] the Arab world remains comparatively silent. To date, the few women to speak openly about their ordeal have been those who reside in the West and write in a language other than Arabic. For example, Lebanese feminist writer Evelyne Accad has published a series of moving articles in diary form that chronicle her journey with breast cancer, but her articles have appeared in English publications such as the quarterly women's journal *Al-Raida* (1994). In recent years, this diary has been published in book form under the title *The Wounded Breast: Intimate Journeys Through Cancer* (2001).

The existing Arabic literature on disability and gender has not only failed to probe the social reality of the disabled female but has not even

12. For further studies on Women and AIDS see Jihane Tawilah (1994).

13. For a comprehensive study of women's cancer literature see Mary K. Deshazer (2005).

provided sufficient data to afford the latter a measure of empirical visibility. It is not possible to assess the literature on disability in the Arab world, Nawaf Kabbara states, without being struck by the "poverty of the intellectual production in the field": most of what is available deals with medical and general issues (2005a, 2). According to Lina Abu-Habib, writing in an introduction to one of the very few books on disability and gender in the Middle East, disabled women in the region "have not been fully integrated in either the disability movement or the women's movement" (1997, 1). To many eyes, it was not until the early 1990s that critical debate into the socio-cultural implications of being disabled began to emerge. This debate was facilitated by the work of the National Association for the Rights of the Disabled in Lebanon (NARD), which has since organized conferences and seminars and published a magazine that caters to Arab individuals with disabilities (Kabbara 2005b, 12).[14] However, it was with the publication of two groundbreaking books in English and Arabic—Lina Abu-Habib's *Gender and Disability* (1997) and Jahda Abou-Khalil's *Nisa' Takhatayna al-Hawajiz: Wahid wa 'Ishrin Sira Dhatiya li Nisa' Tahadayna al-'Aka* (Women Who Crossed the Barriers: The Experiences of Twenty-One Women with Disability in the Arab World) (2001)—that the personal testimonies of disabled women in the region began to appear. From these two lone narratives, one fact emerges again and again out of all the divergent testimonies of women throughout the Arab world: "Cultural norms and social traditions keep [the disabled woman] isolated and marginalized" (Abou-Khalil 2005, 13). Perhaps the most insidious form such marginalization takes is apparently the most benign: a civil and legal emphasis on the rights of women with disabilities to health services, employment, and education comes at the expense of a focus upon their personal experience of their disability. In presuming to speak for, and on behalf of, women with disabilities, the emphasis on civil rights often leaves the women themselves effectively silenced.

14. According to Kabbara, the approach to disability underwent changes at the start of the new century. Except for Lebanon, where disability began to be perceived as a "social and human rights issue" by the late 1980s, the subject of disability only took on a social dimension by the twenty-first century (2005b, 10–12).

This social and cultural marginalization of the physically ill and disabled female body is, as we have already begun to see, every bit as pronounced in narrative fiction as it is in sociological and anthropological discourses on gender, health, and illness. It is remarkable to note that, even in the work of celebrated feminist physician-writers such as Nawal al-Saadawi, the physically sick female has not been provided with sufficient narrative space to articulate her singular experience.[15] Rather, the focus is upon the "social role of medicine and the physician" (Malti-Douglas 1995, 21). To be sure, al-Saadawi's female protagonists resent the "physical peculiarities" of their bodies (Malti-Douglas 1995, 22), but it is not a loathing instigated by a specific physical illness so much as one directed at the sexual and feminine constitution of their bodies which defines them as acquiescent subjects in society.[16] Unsurprisingly, the depiction of female illness in Arabic literature of both male and female writers has revolved around women derailed by psychological disturbances and emotional distress.[17] For any critic seeking to offer a genealogy of the female suffering body in Arabic literature, then, it is necessary to begin with this gesture of marginalization which means that the sick woman only ever appears in her disappearance, only ever becomes visible in her invisibility. If literature—with its unique capacity to enter imaginatively and sympathetically into the lives of others—should be better equipped than any other discourse to embody the sick woman from within, we need to ask why the Arabic novel and short story have, for so much of their history, signally

15. Male writers who also practice medicine have paid more attention to the physically ill male rather than the female. These include: Egyptian Yusuf Idris, Mahmoud Taymur, and Sherif Hetata, and Syrian 'Abd al-Salam al-'Ujayli.

16. An essential example is Nawal al-Saadawi's *Mudhakkirat Tabiba* (*Memoirs of a Woman Doctor*).

17. See, for example, Salwa Bakr's *al-'Araba al-dhahabiya la tas'ad ila al-Sama'* (The Golden Chariot); May Telmissany's *Dunyazad* (Dunyazad); Sahar al-Muji's *Sayyidat al-Manam* (The Dream Woman); Fadia Faqir's *Pillars of Salt*; Elias Khoury's *al-Jabal al-Saghir* (Little Mountain); Hanan al-Shaykh's *Hikayat Zahra* (The Story of Zahra). This is in addition to the overall body of work of Naguib Mahfouz, al-Saadawi, Yusuf Idris, Sahar Khalifeh, and Alia Mamdouh, to name but a few.

failed to rise to meet this challenge. In closing, we also need to consider why (as I have already suggested) the picture may finally be changing today: the female suffering body —so long marginalized—is coming out of the shadows. Why do the modern equivalents of Mahfouz's Amina no longer appear to suffer in silence?

Book Structure

Let me briefly orient the reader toward what follows by giving a chapter-by-chapter breakdown of my argument. Firstly, chapter 1 analyzes the representation of the female suffering body in works by male writers from 1950 to 2000. Chapter 2 explores how women writers depicted female illness and disability during the same period. Chapter 3 focuses on how contemporary male and female writers, publishing their work between 2000 and the present, have sought to effect a transformation in the textual embodiment of female illness and disability. To sketch the overall trajectory of the argument, the study will show that the representation of the female suffering body has been marked by a slow and painful movement from literary invisibility to plain view, from symbolic meaning to lived, corporeal experience, and from a voiceless presence to one that is capable of narrating its own subjective identity. Finally, the conclusion will show that this literary trajectory is paralleled by a historical one, as we will seek to excavate the long-standing stigma associated with imperfect female bodies in the wider Arab imaginary and the changing relationship to ill and disabled female bodies in our contemporary cultural moment.

It will already be apparent that my argument derives its theoretical framework from the medical humanities and, in particular, the sociological and anthropological revolution in the study of health and illness that has taken place over the last few decades. To begin with, a central trope in my thinking will be Michel Foucault's famous analysis of the politics of the gaze in such classic texts as *The Birth of the Clinic* (1973; 1993). For Foucault, in an analysis that extends across *The Birth of the Clinic* (1993), *Discipline and Punish* (1991), and "The Eye of Power" (1980), the politics of the gaze are inseparable from the modern project of disciplining, controlling, and training the individualized body: who sees whom becomes the political question par excellence. In an attempt to extend this argument to a cultural, social, and political sphere with which Foucault himself was largely unfamiliar—the Arab World—I will seek to archaeologize the politics of the gaze as it insinuates itself into the life-world of ill/disabled female characters, the identity of its beholder, and the power relations that are being constructed—in short, the entire discursive production of physically ill/disabled women. Finally, we will see that physically ill and disabled female characters in Arabic literature have just recently begun to materialize because it is only now that the power to gaze—which has for long been directed at female characters who embody ideal, feminine, and sexual attributes—has been conferred upon them.

As the study maps the gradual emergence of the ill female body from the shadows, it will thus also seek to document what Foucault famously calls the nexus of power/knowledge that attaches itself to that body: social, religious and moral stigmas, political and national ideologies, and so on. To be sure, Sontag famously and powerfully argues that we must refrain from reading illness as something other than itself (1990, 1–10), but as we will see in the case of many of the works in question, it is impossible to read illness as anything other than metaphorical: illness becomes a privileged sign of social, political, and ideological otherness. For Mary Douglas and Erving Goffman, in contrast to Sontag, bodies are symbolic carriers of the existing social and political discourse within any given society (1996, 69–87; 1963, 1–35; 1990). If Sontag assumes a basic difference between physical and social bodies, Douglas argues that the relationship between the two is symbiotic: each feeds upon the other and our perception of any one is determined by the other (1996). In light of this debate, the following argument will question the two-way traffic between the corporeal body of the sick female and the social, religious, and body politic of Arab culture more generally.

Finally, what follows will also locate the sick female self within the socio-medical theory of "deviance" that was first introduced by Talcott Parsons's *The Social System* (1951; 1991) and later developed by Eliot Freidson (1970) via a lay referral method. In *The Social System*, Parsons established a correlation between illness and lack of social control by arguing that illness is a form of deviance that renders the ill person incapable of performing the responsibilities allotted to him in the society and which, in turn, frame the identity of the individual in question within the confines of a "sick role" (1991, 280–87). This role legitimizes the need for the sick self to withdraw from social activities in the hope of getting "better." Reading this theory within the framework of the body of Arabic literature under scrutiny, it becomes possible to ask whether sick female characters are assigned equivalent roles within the narratives in question. To what extent is the sick female body "deviant"? Is the invisibility of sick women perpetuated by a sense of legitimized exemption, or do they maintain their functional gendered role within a social structure that refuses to accept their inability to perform? What role do specific illnesses and disabilities, in particular the emphasis on disabilities affecting the legs, play in facilitating or resisting this exclusion?

In summary, then, the physically ill/disabled female body is ultimately too complex and ambivalent to be the subject of one single theoretical perspective. It continually operates (as this introduction has sought to show) at, between, and beyond the boundaries of nature and culture; medicine and sociology; clinical practice; structures of feeling; social, religious and political discourses. To even begin to do justice to this body, we must construct a new theoretical framework that is capable of seeing the body as simultaneously biological, affective, phenomenological, and social—embodied all the way up and constructed all the way down. On the one hand, this study will adopt a social constructionist paradigm that focuses on the sociology of the body more than anything else and whose key exemplars include Foucault, Douglas, Goffman, and Bryan Turner. On the other hand, though, this study will always seek to underpin the constructionist model with an insistence upon the lived corporeal reality of that body itself. If a great deal of the existing literature on health and illness in Arabic literature and culture adopts an "either/or" approach, then, my own framework will be "both/and": we must understand the body (to borrow Helen Marshal's distinctions) as both a corpus of "social interaction" and one that also evolves around "corporeal action" (1999, 71). By reading the female suffering body in Arabic literature both affectively and discursively, we can perhaps begin to bring Amina and her suffering sisters out of the shadows.

1

THE SILENT SUBJECT

Illness and Disability in Male Writing, 1950–2000

In this opening chapter, we will examine the representation of the female suffering body in Arabic literature by male writers between 1950 and 2000. It is important to preface our discussion, though, by reiterating that such representations are remarkably few in number. As we have already hinted at in the Introduction, the story of female illness and disability is largely the story of an absence at the heart of the Arabic novel and short story. Yet, a number of Arab male writers have provided scope for ill bodies and characters to be illuminated, embodied, and represented. For Egyptians Naguib Mahfouz and Yusuf Idris, Lebanese Suhayl Idris, and others, ill and disabled bodies have been the subject of novels and short stories and, in some cases, such bodies are given pivotal roles in the unfolding of the plot, and the expression of larger socio-political ideologies. If such writers do constitute an exception to the rule, though, it is striking to note that almost all of them deal largely with the ill and disabled male body rather than the female one.[1] In those texts that depict the ill female body at all, she is positioned outside the major events of the plot, given minimal narrative voice, and represented in such a highly metaphorical or symbolic fashion as to render the physical dimension of her illness impenetrable.

1. See Naguib Mahfouz's novel *al-Shahhadh* (The Beggar) and his short story "Za'abalawi" (Zaabalawi); Yusuf Idris's short stories "'Ala Asyut" (To Asyut), "Ahmad al-Majlis al-Baladi" (Ahmad of the Local Council), and *Lughat al-Ay Ay* (The Language of Pain).

It is the aim of this chapter to explore what comes to fill the gap where the physically sick female body should be. As the analysis will emphasize, existing male representations of this figure tend to efface its corporeal reality: the sick/disabled female body is little more than the means to explore larger socio-political and religious questions. Perhaps the most visible sign of this textual effacement is that female illness/disability is discursively transformed into (1) a site for a narrative of sin and redemption, (2) a representation of political and national ideologies, and (3) a tool for the affirmation of patriarchal ideologies. By putting the material body into discourse so relentlessly, we might say the corporeal reality of female illness and disability disappears in a puff of signifiers. In rendering the female physical body subsidiary to the social body, Arab male writing thus arguably exemplifies what Nina Baym would see as a form of absence. This is because "the protagonists are both embodied and disembodied," and no matter what attention is given to their sick material body, such attention ultimately "testifies to a spiritual body, a non-body" (1993, xxxviii).

Yet, we will also see that the putting-into-discourse of the material body of this figure in the works of male writers betrays a historic inability to confront physically imperfect female bodies and a resistance to "the problem" of a woman's sexual body, and its role as an active agent in society. As Malti-Douglas notes, the Arabic textual tradition carries with it symptoms of the "problematic nature of woman, her voice, her body . . ." (1991, 67). For Malti-Douglas, medieval Arabic texts produced by men do focus on the corporeality of women, and even allow "the female to participate in this discourse," but the fact remains that, throughout, a woman's "speech remained tied to the seductive power of her body" (1991, 110). In a different sense, what Malti-Douglas calls the "obsess[ion] with the female body" has persisted in the works of modern Arab male writers (1991, 111). This obsession is predominantly with the female sexual body and carries with it a corresponding desexualization, and therefore rejection, of bodies that are deemed imperfect and/or invalid.

This chapter tracks the representation (or more precisely the non-representation) of female physical illness and disability in selected works of Arab male writers from the year 1950 to 2000. Its structure is broadly chronological and thematic. As will become clear, the works analyzed are organized in such a way as to highlight implicit thematic connections among different male writers who touch upon female illness and disability, common configurations and vocabulary they employ in depicting that illness, as well as a consideration of how the historical time period during which they produced their work affected their approach.[2] In order to understand how female illness and disability has emerged from the shadows, we must appreciate why it was marginalized in the first place and this will be the subject of what follows.

Sin and Redemption

One of the most prevalent tropes which Arab male writers deploy to represent female suffering is to transform the latter into a subject of a religious narrative of sin and possible redemption. To begin with, it is important to recognize that the depiction of women in the first and earliest wave of Arabic novels and short stories is already highly constrained. On the one hand, women are passive wives, daughters, and mothers who stay at home and live a mundane, uneventful life. On the other, they are beautiful objects of devotion and worship who are only capable of being appreciated by characters of refined aesthetic sensibilities. In the works of male writers like Tawfiq al-Hakim, Muhammad Husayn Haykal, Taha Husayn, and in the earlier works of Yusuf al-Siba'i, such binary representations predominate.

During the 1940s and 1950s, however, the rise in female education, the proliferation of the number of women who entered the workforce and who became major contributors to the financial stability of the household, particularly in Egypt, had a tremendous impact on the way women were portrayed in Arabic literature. Specifically, the 1950s saw the emergence

2. In some cases, a work that does not fit chronologically is included in a certain section because its subject matter and its thematic framework better locates it within the time period of the other works (by reason of, for example, recounting events within that period). This will be the case with Ziyad Qasim's *Abna' al-Qal'a* which was published in the late 1980s but which will be included in the section that contains an analysis of Kanafani's *Rijal fi al-Shams* that appeared in the early 1960s.

of female characters in Arabic literature. They also brought about more realistic portrayals of female protagonists without completely erasing the previous romantic representations.[3] Yet, according to Miriam Cooke, the attempt to avoid romanticized and idealized images of women meant that literature of the 1950s ended up locking women into a new set of stereotypical representations—first of which was the prostitute or "fallen" woman.[4] In many ways, this was the inevitable patriarchal reaction to the increasing social visibility and empowerment of women in the period. Female characters who wrongly ventured into a still highly masculine public sphere would be damned to remain there by selling their body for money (1987, 74–77).

According to Cooke, then, female characters were thus no longer the "symbol of salvation" that earlier writers had envisioned them to be (1987, 74–77).[5] Yet, in some cases things are not quite so clear-cut: "fallen women" *are* granted salvation and become symbols of moral deliverance in a few works. For Arab male writers of the period, however, such a story of damnation and salvation was principally effected through an illness narrative. In Egyptian Mahmoud Taymur's short story "Wa Usdila al-Sitar" (And the Curtain Is Lowered, 1969), and al-Siba'i's two-volume novel *Nahnu la Nazra'u al-Shawk* (We do not Sow Thorns, 1969), female physical illness becomes the stage for a drama of moral rebirth and redemption.

Mahmoud Taymur: "Wa Usdila al-Sitar"

Published in 1969, Taymur's short story depicts an unnamed sick female protagonist on her deathbed. She reminisces, in an internal monologue,

3. This is most evident in the general works of Mahfouz and writers such as Egyptian 'Abd al-Rahman al-Sharqawi and Yusuf Idris, as well as Syrian Hanna Mina. These writers attempted to construct, with varying degrees, new and realistic portrayals of female characters.

4. For a study of the prostitute figure and the question of prostitution in Arabic literature see Miriam Cooke (1993) and Evelyne Accad (1984).

5. For works that depict female characters as prostitutes see, for example, Mahfouz's *Zuqaq al-Midaq* (Midaq Alley); Fathi Ghanim's *al-Rajul Alladhi Faqada Zillah* (The Man Who Lost His Shadow); Yahya Haqqi's *Qindil Umm Hashim* (Umm Hashem's Lamp).

about her life and the prospect of impending death. During her musings, it is revealed that the protagonist is a spinster whose life was plagued by the continuous struggle to make a living by working as a babysitter. She also fell in love with a man who abandoned her after promising to marry her—hence the life of total isolation thereafter. Along with these experiences, Taymur's story also implies that the woman had committed shameful deeds (without making clear exactly what she has done) to make money and to vent her anger at being deserted by the one man she had loved. In the course of her narrative, the protagonist attributes her sinful actions to falling in with "bad company" who made a living by "stealing money" and "stripping souls," and goes on to emphasize that she submerged herself in that avalanche of "dark living" (Taymur 1969, 113).

At the same time, the story is equally reticent about the precise nature of the woman's illness: we are told that she suffers from a grave illness (the implication being cancer) but we are not given enough physical descriptions to determine definitively what the disease is and, if cancer, of what nature. Yet, in another sense, such knowledge is beside the point, because the psychological and physiological state of the protagonist seems to be rooted entirely in her sinful past. From the outset, the protagonist announces that she has been "punished" by an illness that has sapped her energy "drop by drop" (Taymur 1969, 105). It is one whose "clutches have dug into her exhausted body, left and right," though she has fiercely fought it and spent much on treatment. Nevertheless, the workings of the illness remained merciless and violent (Taymur 1969, 115). In short, Taymur's narrative attaches to the protagonist's illness a whole set of symbolic moral connotations and so the story of her physical decline becomes the story of her moral degeneration and redemption.

Yet another sign that the protagonist's physical illness is connected to her moral condition is the timing of the former's emergence. For just when the protagonist becomes the ideal of pious exhortation, renouncing her past life and embracing a new life of continuous prayer, donating money to the poor, and finally deciding to build a mosque, the illness makes its way into her body. The protagonist claims that she was born and "her page was devoid of that which injures or pleases," then she "lived what she lived and saved what she saved of coins," only to have "fate [inscribe] on the page of her heart what it has inscribed." When the illness finally appears, it is striking that it is depicted not merely as the advent of death but as the possibility of rebirth and rejuvenation. The woman asserts that she is once again becoming an "embryo, decreasing and shrinking slowly. . . ." (Taymur 1969, 116–17). In this debilitating corporeal state, she becomes filled with "the peace of ultimate rest," her soul "rejuvenated as it awaits the moment of salvation," while she is "purified of all transgression and pollution" (Taymur 1969, 107).

For Taymur, then, it is clear that the protagonist's illness is not merely a punishment for past sins but the opportunity for spiritual purification through suffering and death. As the protagonist muses over her life, she also sets her eyes upon an ending which glimmers in the horizon, "brightening" as it comes closer and enabling the woman who is about to die to "drink" the "gluttony and rapture" of death (Taymur 1969, 118). In Lars-Christer Hyden's words, the sickness is here the centrifugal point "from which" all other events are perceived and "to which" all other events are connected (1997, 57). It is also a spiritual liberation that enables the sick subject to "free herself of the captivity of the body" (Taymur 1969, 116).

The physical body represented in "Wa Usdila al-Sitar" is thus intimately connected to the social, moral, and religious body. As Mary Douglas suggests, "the physical experience of the body . . . sustains a particular view of society" because "there is a continual exchange of meanings between the two kinds of bodily experience so that each reinforces the categories of the other" (1996, 68). To return to Taymur's protagonist, it is clear that the woman maintains, throughout her monologue, a relationship to her social and public performance in the past. As the monologue unfolds, the woman's frenzied speech always locates her own bodily pain within a world beyond that body and in an idealized social body with its accompanying demands and pressures. For the protagonist, her current physical decline is consistently located in her social failure to get married: she continuously suggests that, prior to being deserted by the man she had loved, she had been a model of piety, solely dedicated to caring for the offspring of her many employers. In the aftermath of her abandonment by her lover, and with this the loss of any hope of getting married, her pious public performance comes to an end.

This inability to live out her gendered social role also marks the point in the protagonist's life where social deviance begins. It is this deviance that, we have seen, is the symbolic "cause" of her later illness. As such, Taymur's narrative presents a case study in Parsons's groundbreaking theory of the deviant self in sick subjects. Parsons's analysis of sick individuals, recall, sees a correlation between illness and lack of social control by stressing that illness is a kind of "deviant behaviour" or a manifestation of "deviant" performance underlined by an inability to fulfill specific social roles (1991, 285). To this extent, the protagonist's repeated references to her inability to secure a marriage underscores the fact that she has deviated from the social roles expected of women. By the same token, the dramatic change that occurs right after she is abandoned—and that sees her adorning black attire as a manifestation of what she describes as "the mourning of a life" (Taymur 1969, 112)—also witnesses the beginning of her deviance. Perhaps another index of the protagonist's social deviance is the loss of her financial status and, by implication, her moral status as well: she recounts how her suitor stripped her of her life savings and left her deeply indebted (Taymur 1969, 114–15). In both cases, the protagonist's real "illness" is revealed to be her social deviance. Her physical sickness is merely the symptom of this prior and deeper social disfunctionality.

If Taymur's story ultimately locates physical illness in social sickness, the result is that the corporeality of the protagonist's ill body is totally erased. It is possible to argue that this disembodiment even infects the whole first-person narrative, which retains a curiously spectral or abstract quality throughout. At one key moment, for example, the protagonist describes the reluctant young female neighbor who comes regularly to check on her. During these repeated visits, the stranger is always in a hurry to leave. When she leaves, the protagonist recounts that nothing in the room testifies to the stranger's presence, "not even a shadow" (Taymur 1969, 106). To one obvious reading, the spectral stranger's anxiety comes to stand for the general anxiety the story displays toward the female suffering body. The protagonist even imagines her visitor's utter terror at the prospect of finding her dead body. Perhaps, on another level, the absence of any shadow or, more precisely, physical outline of this intruder also signifies the invisibility of all concrete physical bodies—sick or well—within the space of the narrative. In this sense, the impossible physical gap the intruder leaves behind is a highly symbolic one: a kind of ghostly X that marks the spot where the living, corporeal body should have been.

In all these ways, Taymur's "Wa Usdila al-Sitar" occludes the reality of its protagonist's concrete bodily pain and transforms it into a vehicle for a narrative of sin and redemption. The story not only reduces her illness to an abstract state but, more uncomfortably and problematically still, turns her pain into a moral precondition for redemption. Accordingly, the story is best described as a moral, tragic, or even romantic illness narrative in which physical suffering is affirmed as a heroic, transformative, and affirmative fate. For all its attempts to offer a realistic depiction of illness—and the protagonist does speak movingly of her pain, fear, and extreme loneliness—Taymur's story ultimately idealizes her suffering as the terrible price to pay in order to regain virtue at the very end of her life. Perhaps most importantly, it is through the very act of narrating her life story—to herself, to her visitor, and ultimately to the world—that the protagonist's social deviance is left behind and she can re-enter society through her words. In the brief encounters between her and her young neighbor—the one elderly and the other youthful, the one cut off from the world and the other an active part of it, the one whose life is about to end and the other whose life has barely begun—the sick social body begins, however temporarily, to be healed.

Yusuf al-Siba'i: *Nahnu la Nazra'u al-Shawk*

Like Taymur's short story, al-Siba'i's two-volume novel *Nahnu la Nazra'u al-Shawk* belongs to the genre of the moral illness narrative. Also published in 1969, the novel focuses on the tragic life of a lower-class, uneducated female protagonist, Sayyida, who is repeatedly denied the social respectability she most desires. Sayyida struggles to rise above her dismal social and economic status but marries dishonest men and is deserted by them. Most devastatingly, she is deprived of her only son. In telling Sayyida's story, al-Siba'i also tells the story of her social class and the injustices that class suffers.

It is not enough, though, to say that *Nahnu la Nazra'u al-Shawk* is simply a story about social class in Egypt, because, parallel to that narrative is also the story of one woman's illness. After all, the novel—like "Wa Usdila al-Sitar"—begins with Sayyida reclining on a bed, sick, and on the verge of death. During this last phase of her life she revisits her past, recounting a series of personal experiences that, to borrow Kleinman's description of end-of-life narratives, need to be "tidied up, put in their proper place, rethought and, equally important, retold in what can be regarded as a story rapidly approaching its end" (1988, 49–50). The description of the final stage of Sayyida's chronic illness is once again conducted in the moral, romantic terms that seem to characterize illness narratives of the period. By transforming physical illness into a story of moral degeneration and possible redemption, *Nahnu la Nazra'u al-Shawk* is once again complicit in the marginalization of the physically ill female body in favor of the ill social body.

For the dying Sayyida, illness brings not only a wasting of the body but also peace and liberation from a painful life. In her transition from a young, innocent girl raised by a cruel stepmother to a mature woman whose sole aim is to raise a family of her own, Sayyida finds that her (poignantly modest) dreams are unattainable by honest or "respectable" means. To survive economically and socially, she is forced to become a prostitute and to suffer a host of other miseries: she is raped, exploited by men, and becomes the mistress of a married man before returning to prostitution. When Sayyida narrates the story of her life, she not only recounts her personal history but also evaluates it.

Despite being a first-person narrative, larger questions of moral worth, public and private performances of gender, and redemption via illness are once again integral to her self-understanding. Put simply, Sayyida's story is not merely a personal narrative but one that is socially produced and determined by the dominant patriarchal ideology. Just as with Taymur's "Wa Usdila al-Sitar," it is the female protagonist's illness that becomes the privileged site where personal experience and social environment come together.

To begin with, the timing of Sayyida's illness, just like in "Wa Usdila al-Sitar," exemplifies the moralized and gendered nature of the illness itself along with its redemptive capacity. After a life of battling in the public sphere to survive, and after witnessing the death of her young son,

Sayyida hits rock bottom. However, fate extends a sympathetic hand by finding her a safe haven in the house of a family that had once sheltered her when she was young and whose head of the household, Hamdi al-Samaduni, is the one man she had always loved. There, Sayyida lives and cares for the house and becomes a second mother to Hamdi's son, Muhammad. Perhaps most crucially, she becomes Sayyidat al-bayt: mistress of the house. In this moment of redemption, though, Sayyida's health is disrupted by the appearance of a malignant tumor in her stomach.

Like in "Wa Usdila al-Sitar," the emergence of the sickness at this stage of the protagonist's life is the signifier of a patriarchal ideology of ideal and fallen womanhood. Sayyida's illness strikes at a time when she has retreated to the private domain and, in this sense, has been restored to her "rightful" social position by fulfilling the traditional gendered performance society dictates. If the protagonist of "Wa Usdila al-Sitar" begins to redeem herself through religious rituals, Sayidda's redemption commences not only with the movement from the public to the private domain but also with the devotional exercise of motherhood. The maternal bonds that Sayyida develops with Hamdi's son redeem her "failure" to be a mother to her biological son. All her past misdeeds are overcome in the process of establishing an alternative maternal world in the house of her employers. Sayyida begins to feel that God has granted her a "safe and decent place," where the head of the house treats her like a rightful member of it, buying her headscarves, cotton bras, and food for the birds whenever she requests them (al-Siba'i 1969, 1:12). In another sense, of course, the fact that Sayyida requests these gifts in particular is far from coincidental: they signify her moral transformation from a woman who sells her body to one who protects it by desexualizing herself with plain, modest attire.

The moment when Sayyida's traditional gender role in society is restored is also the moment that she succumbs to illness. Yet, the latter only leaves her at peace with the world, because with illness comes the prospect of death, which, in her view, is the final confirmation of her restoration to the domestic sphere. To underscore this point, Sayyida asks that she be buried in her employer's family graveyard. When the doctor wishes to admit her to hospital, the reader learns that her surrogate son does not accept this recommendation. More importantly, Sayyida herself rejects the idea and chooses to embrace the traditional idea that her position is within the house, not outside it. In the family debate over Sayyida's ill body—and in particular over whether it belongs in the private or the public sphere—we see the larger debate over the visibility of female illness in the period.

If, in one sense, Sayyida's illness resists entry into the public sphere, we might argue that, in another sense, it has always already been there because it is so thoroughly permeated by moral, social, and religious discourse. Her physical suffering is once again romanticized as the prerequisite for moral transformation. Like the protagonist of "Wa Usdila al-Sitar," Sayyida almost embraces her illness and makes little effort to seek treatment. Rather, she opts to "raise the white flag" for death (al-Siba'i 1969, 2:937). In the process of physical decline, she has apparently been purified: Sayyida believes "God will honor her" with an appropriate burial site in her afterlife (al-Siba'i 1969, 2:937).

This spiritualization of illness becomes particularly clear in the final scene of the novel, which depicts Sayyida lying on her bed with "colorful birds humming in the cage" beside her (al-Siba'i 1969, 2:942). She asks her surrogate son to open the cage door so the birds can fly to freedom (al-Siba'i 1969, 2:945). Yet, what might seem at first glance to be a symbolic call for women's social and economic liberation turns out to be the desire for a very different kind of "freedom": the flight of the birds is a symbol of Sayyida's soul, armored with religious faith, flying into the arms of death. In her dying words, it seems that she has finally achieved the freedom she could not attain in life. We are told that "suddenly the pain disappeared," and Sayyida was no longer a "slave to her needs, or her feelings or her sadness or her pain" (al-Siba'i 1969, 2:946).[6]

6. It is interesting to note that comparatively recent male writing continues to emphasize the moral and the spiritual dimension of female illness narratives. One example is Hanna Mina's *Hamama Zarka' fi al-Suhub* (A Blue Pigeon in the Horizon, 1988). The illness of the female protagonist becomes the means toward a deep redemption. In this instance, however, the redemptive focus is upon her father: it is through bearing witness to the illness of his daughter that the father is able to redeem himself, and by extension, patriarchy

Domestic Bodies, National Subjects

In addition to seeing female illness and disability in moral or religious terms, Arab male writing of the period also transforms the female body into a symbol of the state of the nation: the ill or disabled female body becomes the privileged sign of the sick, wounded, or fractured nation. As George Tarabishi affirms, women in Arabic novels have always served as representations of the nation: Tarabishi's analysis draws mainly on the works of Egyptian writers such as Tawfiq al-Hakim's *'Awdat al-Ruh* (Return of the Spirit, 1932), Mahfouz's *Miramar* (Miramar, 1967), Fathi Ghanim's *Tilka al-Ayyam* (Those Days, 1966), and *Zaynab wa al-'Arsh* (Zainab and the Throne, 1977; Tarabishi 1981). In an analysis of the impact of socio-political and cultural changes upon the Arabic novel, Sabry Hafez also discusses the shifts in the representation of the nation/country in relation to Arab female literary heroines.

For Hafez, the pre-1960 Arabic novel was principally concerned with resisting colonial occupation. Hence, internal divisions within and between the various Arab states were minimized in an effort to imaginatively unite the Arab nation against an external occupier. The Arab nation, Hafez argues, was often identified with the image of a familiar, peasant girl with a gentle, loving temperament. This was particularly evident in Haykal's *Zaynab* (1913), al-Sharqawi's *al-Ard* (Egyptian Earth, 1954), and Mahfouz's *Miramar.* In a few cases, the country was represented as an urban woman but, even then, this woman remained an "idealized girl from the very popular quarter of the city in which the rural ethos was very much alive": this was particularly apparent in al-Hakim's *'Awdat al-Ruh* and its heroine Saniyya (Hafez 1994, 94).

However, in the period after the 1960s, explains Hafez, more educational opportunities unfolded, greater "social mobility" became available, and patriarchal influence weakened. Simultaneously, "socio-cultural awareness" intensified and this perpetuated a heightened sense of one's

more generally. I have chosen not to include this novel because the female protagonist is represented as a child rather than a woman.

identity and "difference from others." This resulted in "social unrest, sectarian violence and even civil war." The image of the country in the literature of the time became embodied by the "middle-class urban woman." For Hafez, examples of this include Egyptian Latifa al-Zayyat's *al-Bab al-Maftuh* (The Open Door, 1960), Iraqi Fuad al-Takarli's *al-Raj'al-Ba'id* (The Long Way Back, 1980), and Syrian Haydar Haydar's *Walima li-a'Shab al-Bahr* (A Banquet for Seaweed, 1979; Hafez 1994, 94–95).[7]

Perhaps, though, there is an additional, and until now largely neglected, female trope for the representation of the Arab nation: the disabled female character. To be sure, disability has often served as "an opportunistic metaphorical device" in literary narratives throughout history (Mitchell and Snyder 2000, 47). It has also "played host to a panoply of other social maladies that writers seek to address" (Mitchell 2002, 17). Writing on the representation of female disability during the nineteenth century, critics such as Cindy LaCom have even noted that the majority of these disabled bodies are in fact female. Yet, interestingly, Arabic literature seems to be an exception to this textual rule: the representation of disability as a metaphor and even a material reality has been restricted and/or limited to male protagonists, while female disability has remained largely absent.[8] In fact, we find female disability as a symbol of the nation in only two major texts: Palestinian Ghassan Kanafani's *Rijal fi al-Shams* and Jordanian Ziyad Qasim's *Abna' al-Qal'a*.

7. For studies on gender and nationalism in the Arab world more generally see, for example, Margot Badran (1995); Elizabeth Thompson (2000); Beth Baron (2005); Lisa Pollard (2005).

8. In Arabic narratives about the nation-state, disabled male protagonists in both fiction and film have been, in some instances, cast as heroes of the national struggle, and their disability has been seen as a marker of this heroism. To take one example, in Egyptian Ahmad Badrakhan's film *Allah Ma'ana* (God Is with Us, 1955), which focuses on the 1952 Egyptian revolution, the male lead character is wounded during a national battle and loses an arm. Yet, his disability is applauded and even legitimizes his participation in the plight of the nation. In the following section, we will see that this is certainly not the case with representations of female disability.

Ghassan Kanafani: *Rijal fi al-Shams*

Published in 1962, *Rijal fi al-Shams* (Men in the Sun) is one of Kanafani's most pessimistic works. It also established his reputation as a leading Arab writer whose work did not solely express political commitment but also a sophisticated narrative technique and a subtle thematic vision. According to Muhammad Siddiq, the recognition that *Men in the Sun* received was prompted by its "narrative technique . . . the haunting symbolic significance with which its action resonate[d], and its apocalyptic vision of Palestinian reality" (1984, 9–10). To briefly summarize the plot, the novella tells the story of three Palestinian refugees—Abou-Qais, As'ad, and Marwan—who struggle to cross a desert that extends from Iraq to Kuwait in order to improve their bleak livelihoods in the latter country. But lacking any means to pay Iraqi smugglers, the three refugees agree to be smuggled by a fourth Palestinian, Abou al-Khayzaran, in a truck for a smaller amount of money. A condition of the agreement is that they agree to hide in the truck's tank at border checkpoints. The men survive the fierce heat and airlessness of the tank when crossing the first checkpoint, but at the second Abou al-Khayzaran is detained by interrogators. When he is finally set free, Abou al-Khayzaran returns to the truck to discover that his three passengers have suffocated to death. Abou al-Khayzaran is then depicted getting rid of the three corpses after taking their money from their pockets.

To be sure, *Men in the Sun* is an exceptionally bleak narrative: what begins as a hopeful journey toward a more prosperous future for displaced Palestinians only leads to their deaths. It is also a narrative that resists any possibility of change for the Palestinian people whether individually or collectively. After all, the deaths of the three men reflect the "collective symbolic status" of Palestinians whose fate has left them incapable of "perpetuating the Palestinian species" (Siddiq 1984, 13),[9] insofar as they are incapable of finding a place and a territory in which to

9. While Abou al-Khayzaran survives, Siddiq argues that his own physical disability means that there is no possibility of extending the life of the Palestinian people.

survive.[10] If Kanafani's story has principally been read in political terms, though, the narrative also weaves other stories, events, and characters into the master narrative via the main protagonists' recollections. In the particular context of this book, the most pertinent of these minor characters is the disabled Shafiqa whose presence dramatizes yet another discourse and representation of female physical illness and disability in the works of Arab male writers during the 1950s and 1960s.

As Marwan recalls the circumstances that led him to seek a new life in Kuwait, we are introduced to the character of Shafiqa. Marwan recounts that he has undertaken the perilous journey in order to make enough money to support his mother and siblings, all of whom were deserted by a father who left his family to marry someone else. His father marries the other woman, Shafiqa, not out of love but because of the social and financial security she offers. To begin with, Marwan claims he cannot understand how his father abandoned his mother for "no reason than to marry that deformed woman." Later, though, he admits that his father was desperate to "move from the mud house which he had occupied in the camp" for years and to spend his remaining years "under a concrete roof"—dreams that marriage to Shafiqa could at least help become real. Shafiqa owns a proper house and lives off money provided to her by charity. The money reassures Marwan's father that he could "live out the rest of his life in security, untroubled by anything" (Kanafani 1978, 26). But, as Kanafani's narrative suggests, this attainment of financial and social stability comes with a hefty price: Shafiqa's disability. The manner in which this disability is described once again dramatizes the social stigma attached to physically invalid women in the Arab world. In a larger sense, though, we will see that Shafiqa is also the embodiment of a stigmatized nation.

What characterizes the disabled body of Shafiqa in *Men in the Sun*? Firstly, what is most striking is, once again, her invisibility: her own voice is largely omitted even in Marwan's recollections, while the textual descriptions of her are brief. Yet, it is in what is left largely unspoken that

10. See Barbara Harlow (1996).

a discourse on female physical illness and disability is revealed. According to one perspective, Shafiqa's relative invisibility emphasizes the level of social exclusion and shame that her imperfect physical state prompts in her culture. The language that Marwan uses to describe her stresses her social and moral alterity. In his discourse, there is something even freakish or monstrous about his father's new wife.

Shafiqa, according to Marwan, is a woman whose leg had been "amputated at the top of the thigh," leaving her as a "burden" to her own father and a repulsive woman to men in general (Kanafani 1978, 26). Her attractive facial features are not sufficient to convince anyone to marry her. If anything, her physical state has transformed her "beautiful" face into a "hard-featured" one that resembles the faces of "all those who are incurably ill." Even "her lower lip was twisted" in a manner that indicated she was "about to cry" (Kanafani 1978, 29). The fact that someone like her is able to secure a man, even one as old as Marwan's father, strikes Marwan as totally incomprehensible. In short, Shafiqa is a "deformed woman" whose physical imperfections are, to society, signifiers of an imperfect character as well (Kanafani 1978, 25).

It is important to note that Shafiqa's disability is always presented via the perception of others, specifically Marwan, and never through her own self-perceptions. At the same time, Marwan's perceptions are colored by his own hardly neutral or impartial perspective on events. For Sander L. Gilman, writing on Western illness narratives, illness has repeatedly been represented as an "Other" in this manner: it is always the other person who is ill, sick, disabled. Gilman argues that the "fear of collapse" and "the sense of dissolution which contaminated the Western image of all diseases" lie behind the representation of illness and disease. Yet this "fear does not remain internalized" but is "projected onto the world in order to localize it and, indeed, to domesticate it." This is because, according to Gilman, "once we locate it, the fear of our own dissolution is removed. Then it is not we who totter on the brink of collapse but rather the other. And it is an Other who has already shown his or her own vulnerability by having collapsed" (1988, 1). In Marwan's depiction of Shafiqa's disability (perceived as an illness), we can see precisely this process of othering at work.

The dominant mood in *Men in the Sun* is one of desolation, as the three main characters are gradually stripped of their self-worth, dignity, and hope. When Marwan describes Shafiqa, he projects onto her body all the disenchantments, wounds, and sense of victimhood that assail him. The allusions to Shafiqa's lips twitching in a manner akin to crying, her arms raised upward in a gesture of prayer, and her features being tainted with the mark of untreatable illness are all a reflection of the vulnerable physical and psychological state of the protagonists, particularly Marwan. In this respect, Shafiqa's disability is merely a symptom of Marwan's own intense physical and psychic vulnerability.

Perhaps, in a larger sense, we might also argue that Shafiqa's body also symbolizes the social and political body of Palestine itself. It is not merely the peasant girl or the urban woman who comes to stand in for the Arab nation but also the disabled female body. The brief disability/illness narrative we can decode through Marwan's description of Shafiqa can also be interpreted as a "state of the nation" narrative about a people in crisis. Just as Abou al-Khayzaran's loss of his physical manhood, together with his failure to help the other three Palestinians, has been perceived as both a symbol of the failure of Palestinian leadership at the time and an ironic critique of the discourse of pan-Arab nationalism, so one can read Shafiqa as a symbol of the broken Palestinian nation.[11] In this respect, Shafiqa inhabits a position in the narrative that is every bit as metaphorically and symbolically potent as that of the major male characters.

The fact that Shafiqa's disability was caused by a "bombardment of Jaffa" (Kanafani 1978, 26), rather than natural causes, immediately places her on the same level as men like Abou al-Khayzaran, who, we are told, lost his manhood because of an injury inflicted during a battle in 1948. Just as Abou al-Khayzaran's castration symbolizes the loss of nationhood,[12] so

11. Here, Abou al-Khayzaran is also an exception to representations of the disabled male whose impairment is generally applauded in discourses on the nation-state. Perhaps this is because his disability is related to his masculine identity and hence he is not perceived as fully male.

12. On the other hand, Abou-Qais is a symbol of past Palestine and a reminder of peasant life as well as attachment to the land. See Mary N. Layoun (1990).

Shafiqa's amputated limbs reinforce the physical costs that accompanied the loss of the nation. In both a literal and a symbolic sense, Shafiqa's body overlaps with that of her nation: she both carries the mark of the wounded nation and is herself an embodiment of it.

While Shafiqa's immobility is yet another metaphor of the overall inertia of Palestinian livelihood, her inability to move also parallels the ironic fate of the three Palestinians who leave behind their homeland and seek a prosperous future home that, increasingly, seems to reside in the realm of fantasy. The men in Kanafani's novel have no way of gaining agency over their lives except through mobility, but their journey takes them no further than Shafiqa's disabled body can carry her. If the journey toward a new beginning in *Men in the Sun* is one ironic parable about the fate of the Palestinians, then the inert body of Shafiqa is another: it offers an alternative symbolic repository for the collective misery of Palestinian history as well as a dark prophecy that the future will not be any brighter. In this sense, Kanafani's narrative transforms both male and female bodies into icons for a nation reduced to a ghastly parody of its original self.

If Shafiqa's body is a metaphor for a wounded nation, though, this same body can also be read as the symbolic antithesis of the nation/homeland: the place of refuge. It could be argued (although Kanafani's text does not seem particularly interested in following this possibility through) that she becomes a symbolic refugee camp for those displaced from their homeland nation. When Marwan's father marries Shafiqa, it is striking that her body becomes synonymous with the house that she owns. Marwan's father agrees to marry Shafiqa because she gives him a roof over his head. To marry the disabled Shafiqa enables him to live the last days of his life with the minimal level of dignity the house provides. For both Marwan's father and Shafiqa herself, her disability becomes a commodity that can be exchanged for the social and economic security that all the male characters in the novel are so desperate to gain. In her physical weakness, Shafiqa is ironically more powerful, and more able to afford security and protection, than public figures like Abou al-Khayzaran.

Shafiqa's house can, thus, be read as a symbolic version of the place of refuge that all Palestinians searched for after being driven out of their homes. It is important to note here that the house is not merely a dwelling place for Marwan's father: Shafiqa also offers to shelter Marwan's mother and her children. Just as the camps were made possible because of humanitarian efforts to shelter Palestinians in exodus, Shafiqa's house was purchased by money provided to her by charity because of her disability. In ironic contrast to the tank where the main characters die so miserably, Shafiqa's house is a genuine place of refuge, if only for one Palestinian man.

This potentially more positive counter-reading of Shafiqa's body and her place in Palestinian society must, however, be seen against the backdrop of a narrative that generally consigns her to the margins. It is striking, for instance, that the surrogate home that Shafiqa offers Marwan's father resides on "the edge of town" (Kanafani 1978, 26), in the same way that her disabled body is located on the fringes of society. At the same time, the fact that Shafiqa's appeal is entirely connected to her economic value is clearly an inverse sign of her physical unworthiness in the eyes of the men. For Marwan and the other men in the community Shafiqa can only truly be valuable in herself if she is able to play the traditional female role of mother. Her apparent inability to have children further undermines her value not only to her husband but to the Palestinian nation as a whole. In this respect, Kanafani's novel is already anticipating what we saw in the Introduction to be an emerging biopolitical debate surrounding the role of mothers in Palestinian nation-building: biological reproduction is not merely a personal right but a political duty to sustain the Palestinian people.

In later decades, the question of population—and particularly of maintaining high fertility rates among Palestinian families inside and outside the country—would increasingly come to be seen as a "potent weapon" in the Palestinian-Israeli conflict (Fargues 2000, 468). For Palestinian leaders, fertility thus became both personally and politically a matter of life and death: either "maintaining the status quo or regaining a status quo ante" (Fargues 2000, 446). By this logic, Palestinian women became (again quite literally) the mothers of the nation and key players in its struggle. Yet, *Men in the Sun* subverts any potential employment of women as national symbols and embodiments of the land itself. It is no coincidence that this marriage of convenience between a disabled woman and an old man, who simply wishes to escape, is, apparently, a childless one. In this sub-narrative, just as in the main narrative, *Men in the Sun* predicts that the only real future for the Palestinian people will be death.

Ziyad Qasim: *Abna' al-Qal'a*

If Kanafani's *Men in the Sun* emerges out of the traumatic process of Palestinian displacement from the homeland after 1948, Jordanian writer Qasim's historical novel *Abna' al-Qal'a* (Sons of the Castle)[13]—which was completed in 1988 and published in 1990—returns to the same events from the perspective of Palestinians displaced to Jordan.[14] In Qasim's 422-page work, he tells the story of the Palestinian experience from the time of the Nakba through the ensuing years of displacement and resistance, all the way up to the June 1967 defeat.

It is through the story of one particular family that Qasim chooses to refract this larger narrative. As *Abna' al-Qal'a* intertwines personal tragedies with national ones, it progressively exposes the personal, social, and economic cost of the Palestinian struggle. To be more precise still, Qasim's novel seeks to embody that trauma in the body of one of its female protagonists: the disabled daughter Fawziya. Just as *Men in the Sun* turns Shafiqa into the embodiment of a wounded nation, so *Abna' al-Qal'a* transforms the suffering body of a woman into a signifier of a traumatized nation. And again like Kanafani's novella, Qasim's novel ultimately leaves the female disabled body silent and invisible.

The novel tells the story of a Circassian family in Amman forced to confront a series of tragic events that erupt after a car accident leaves one of its female members and her husband dead and the second female member, Fawziya, without a leg. Devastated by the aftermath of this accident,

13. All quotes are from the third edition (1998).

14. Although this book does not belong to the same time period as *Men in the Sun,* Fahd Salameh argues that Jordanian writers in the 1980s "were a continuation of the trend that dominated [Arabic] novel writing" of the 1960s and 1970s. As such, most of the Jordanian novels of the 1980s were "no different" from previous works in technique and structure and, as Qasim's novel shows, subject matter (2000, 170).

Shamsuddine—the father of the two women and the head of the household—retreats from society to mourn the death of his first daughter and the disfigurement of the second. In this state of desolation, he rejects all displays of life—including communication with Fawziya.

After the lonely death of Shamsuddine, Fawziya and her brother Fakhri are left alone: Fawziya is charged with taking care not only of Fakhri but of her two nephews, whose parents died during the fateful accident. The boys are raised by Fawziya in their maternal grandparents' home, as if they are her own children. In the remainder of the text, Qasim moves on to chronicle the developing relationships between these individuals, specifically Fawziya and her nephews, and local and national political groups such as the Ba'ath Socialist Party and the Nasserite Movement.

On the one hand, the novel can be read on a purely personal level as the story of Fawziya, "a woman who never got married, but performs the role of a mother for three boys." On the other, it can be perceived from a wider angle as a narrative about "the interrelationships between different social, economical and political arenas in states of alliance and confrontation" (Salameh 2000, 177–78). Yet whatever reading one adopts, the story of Fawziya's disability haunts both the domestic and the national arena. In Fawziya's disabled body, we find another metaphor of the wounded nation as well as the lingering sense of shame female disability triggers in Arab cultures, even when these domestic bodies are transformed into national subjects.

To be sure, Fawziya's loss of her leg dramatically transforms not only the course of her life but that of her family. Her father and fiancé prove to be incapable of dealing with what appears to them as her physical ruin. Instead of comforting Fawziya, they shun her and effectively force her to console them for their own trauma. During the period that Fawziya spends in the hospital recuperating from the accident that left one of her legs "crushed to the bones" (Qasim 1998, 18), her fiancé only visits her three times, the third time coming to break his engagement to her "quickly and calmly." As a result of this separation, Fawziya returns to her father's house a deserted, single woman walking on a set of crutches which cause her to feel "regret and anger and despair" (Qasim 1998, 19). In spite of these few words concerning her post-traumatic state, Fawziya's subjectivity is never explored in any detail throughout the novel except negatively: it is predicted that she will never marry and have children of her own.

Rather, it is the emotional impact of Fawziya's injury upon her family, and in particular her father Shamsuddine, that Qasim chooses to explore. The narrator recounts that in an act of "mercy" Fawziya puts her own process of mourning to the side and returns to taking care of the house and her father. By doing so, she erects a shield to protect her against the trauma of her physical body and her abject social state. However, even this is not enough to dispel her father's revulsion at her disability. The man continues to be haunted by the sound of "that wooden leg"—so much so that Fawziya implores him to stop "weakening her" with his abstinence from food, communication, and life itself (Qasim 1998, 20). In this sense, Fawziya's amputated limb—whose absence is made all the more conspicuous by its prosthetic replacement—becomes an uncanny reminder of Shamsuddine's overall sense of loss.

The loss is at once personal and collective, revealing once again the overlap between individual and national tragedies in the novel. Shamsuddine's failure to prevent the accident destroys his self-image as an all-powerful patriarch. It also destroys the illusion that the domestic space is a refuge from the external traumas of the Palestinian national tragedy: the amputation of Fawziya's leg reminds her father that the society in which he exists is filled with suffering and that he is neither immune to nor cut off from it. In the form of her lost limb, Palestine's dismemberment is written on Fawziya's body for all to see.

Yet, as we have seen throughout this chapter, Fawziya's disability becomes visible only in its invisibility and appears only in its textual disappearance. According to Brody's take on sickness stories, Fawziya's disability deprives her of her traditional "social role" of wife and mother and leaves her in a "liminal" space. This position of "limbo" means that she is unable to participate in the "social interactions between the able-bodied" persons around her (Brody 2003, 154). To gain any sense of interaction with her father, Fawziya is forced to suppress her own trauma and console him. She has what Robert Murphy calls "a duty to comfort others about the others discomfort in confronting [her] disability" (1990, 107). Despite Fawziya's consolation, her father perceives her disability as a punishment from God against him because he had, just before the accident, contemplated marrying a sixteen-year-old girl. Though he had been a fearless warrior who fought against the Turks and the French (Qasim 1998, 15), after the accident Fawziya's father withdraws from society and spends his last days as a feeble figure who needs to be bathed and fed. The conviction that Fawziya's disability was caused by the reckless desire of the head of the household further affirms the discourse of stigma that is associated with female physical disability. In a deeper sense, it is also a way of occluding the physical fact of that disability even more: Fawziya's body is no longer her own but the sign of divine vengeance against her father.

For Qasim, then, just as for Kanafani before him, the interior subjectivity of the disabled female body remains at best a marginal, liminal presence in the body of the text. It is, as we have already begun to see, transformed from a concrete female body into the symbolic embodiment of a wounded nation. After all, it is scarcely coincidental that Qasim's description of the accident in which Fawziya is maimed is immediately followed by a description of the Palestinian national tragedy of 1948: the massive number of displaced Palestinians arriving in Amman adds "an existence to [the city's] existence" (Qasim 1998, 20). In other word's, Fawziya's accident becomes an uncanny harbinger of the fate of the nation. The Palestinian body politic undergoes the same process of trauma, dismemberment, and disintegration as this young woman.

Perhaps this parallel between the traumatized body of Fawziya and that of Palestine itself becomes even clearer at the end of the novel. It concludes with yet another Arab national crisis: Nasser's defeat in the 1967 War with Israel. During this war, Fawziya's house collapses after being bombed in an Israeli attack, and the woman's second leg is injured. Tragically, the doctors assert that they have to amputate the leg. The reaction of Faris, Fawziya's nephew, to this news underscores the extent to which Fawziya's wounded body is a symbolic representation of the wounds of the nation. In response to the doctors' demand, the young man passionately declares: "You do not know what Fawziya is? You do not know who Fawziya is? She is not a mortal who dies nor a body that decays. She is an entity, she is a sentiment, she is a homeland. Do homelands die? And can parts of a homeland be cut off? Amputate her legs. Amputate her hands.

She will remain Fawziya. Help her to live!" (Qasim 1998, 411). By raising Fawziya's body to the position of the body politic, Faris totally erases the physicality of that body in favor of its symbolic value: she is Palestine.

The elevation of the disabled female body into the national symbol par excellence also contains an implicit admission that the trope of the vigorous male body no longer speaks to a nation in crisis. It is no accident that, just like in *Men in the Sun*, the masculine construction of the nation is rendered flaccid and immobile in *Abna' al-Qal'a*. As Abou al-Khayzaran fails in his national responsibility toward the three Palestinians, so Fawziya's father is symbolically stripped of his national role when he withdraws from the world in grief: his miserable death at the beginning of the novel is a clear sign of what will ensue on a political level later on. Yet, as Shamsuddine abandons all individual and national responsibilities, it is Fawziya, significantly, who takes them up. By raising her two nephews, who were themselves displaced from Palestine, she becomes not only the foster mother to her sister's children but provides them with the alternative home and homeland they have lost. She also performs acts of charity for the poor and needy. In spite of her own lack of children, Fawziya becomes a real and a symbolic mother to her community and society.

If Fawziya's position in the overall narrative becomes ever more central, however, her disability increasingly retreats to the margins. It is as if she possesses every quality—kindness, goodness, generosity—except a body. Moreover, the men in her life continually avoid any mention of her disability, as if there were a silent family pact to pretend it does not exist. Every time they speak of Fawziya, they highlight only her spiritual and psychological qualities. In conversation with his friends, for example, Faris boasts that Fawziya is "a great woman"—but he refuses to answer when asked why his aunt never married. Only the sad look on his face betrays any hint of Fawziya's condition (Qasim 1998, 157). This small moment of silence is symptomatic of the larger silence toward female physical disability that haunts the novel.

In its simultaneous elevation of Fawziya to a symbol of the nation and reduction of her to a silent and invisible subject, Qasim's novel perfectly dramatizes the tension toward the female suffering body in male Arabic literature. On the one hand, the disabled woman becomes a new and powerful metaphor for the Arab nation in crisis. But, on the other, the narrative refuses to let go of the discourse of stigma or shame that the imperfect female body provokes. By raising Fawziya to the status of a national symbol, the novel erases all trace of corporeality: she can only embody the nation by, ironically, becoming disembodied in her very physicality. Yet, the fact of that physical stigma still seeps through to undermine every attempt to transform the domestic physical body into a symbolic national subject. Finally, the body of Fawziya becomes an ambiguous site upon which both new political discourses of nationhood, on the one hand, and lingering social discourses of stigma and taboo, on the other, are bodied forth endlessly.

Devotional Wives, Docile Women

A third strategy by which female physical illness and disability is rendered invisible in Arab male writing is to situate the female character entirely within the parameters of the domestic sphere and traditional gender roles. This strategy demands that the sick protagonist performs and experiences her illness in line with the patriarchal notion of what womanhood is and how women should live it, even when experiencing physical, social, and psychological burdens. As we will see, the two dominant female roles at play here are the docile wife and the sacrificing mother. While the previous section highlighted how female illness and disability become metaphors for the state of the nation, this section seeks to locate female physical illness in "domesticity and domestic fiction" (Herndl 1993, 29).[15] In what follows, I will particularly focus on the sick female in Mahfouz's *al-Sukkariya*, the third in his Cairo trilogy, and in Syrian Hanna Mina's semi-autobiographical work *Baqaya Suwar.*

Naguib Mahfouz: *al-Sukkariya*

Mahfouz's Cairo trilogy *Bayn al-Qasrayn, Qasr al-Shawq, al-Sukkariya* (Palace Walk, Palace of Desire, and Sugar Street), written between 1947 and

15. Diane Price Herndl uses this category in her discussion of female illness in American fiction, but the term can be applied in this instance to the works in the ensuing section.

1952, then published in 1956–1957, is perhaps the most widely read work of Arab fiction, both regionally and internationally. The trilogy, which unfolds between the years 1914 and 1944, chronicles the story of three generations of a middle class Egyptian family headed by the inflexible patriarch Sayyid 'Abd al-Jawad. In each volume, the story of the Jawad family is recounted against the backdrop of the massive social and political transformations in Egyptian society during the period.

It is hardly surprising that a trilogy that depicts what happens when traditional Egyptian culture meets an "intrusive alien and materialist civilization advancing from the West" (Le Gassick 1991, 3) should also have much to say about the status of women. Yet, what is perhaps more surprising is that the third volume of the trilogy, *al-Sukkariya* (Sugar Street),[16] also confronts the sick female body in the character of 'Abd al-Jawad's wife, Amina. In its representation of Amina's experience with illness, Mahfouz's text exemplifies another prevalent trope in Arab male writing on female illness and disability: the figure of the angelic, sick mother/wife.

We first meet Amina in the earliest volume of the trilogy *Palace Walk*. She is portrayed as a gentle, innocent, and passive wife and mother who embodies all the patriarchal ideals of womanhood. Her world revolves around the household that her husband rules with an iron will. The only time Amina ever defies the authority of her husband is when, upon the encouragement of her children, she ventures outside the house to visit the shrine of a holy figure (1990).

As we saw in the Introduction, religious pilgrimages play a significant empowering role in the lives of Arab women, particularly those afflicted by illness. For Fatima Mernissi, such "visits to and involvement with saints and sanctuaries are two of the rare options left women *to be*, to shape their world and their lives" (1977, 104). By the same token, Inhorn has observed that the "pilgrimages to saints' tombs allow women to reaffirm, if only temporarily, control over their lives . . . through actions that are autonomous from men" (1994, 221). In the same way, Amina's visit to

16. All quotes are from the translated text, *Sugar Street* (1992).

the shrine is her only "exclusive female activity" (Inhorn 1994, 221)—yet the repercussions of this modest action are severe.

During that fateful journey, Amina breaks a leg and the truth of her disobedience is discovered by the head of the household who, after she recuperates, punishes her severely by dismissing her from the house and only lets her back when neighbors and friends intercede on her behalf. In the character of Amina, then, Mahfouz provides a portrait of middle class women in Egypt at the start of the twentieth century and introduces what Hafez calls "a subtle layer of narrative that steadily subverts patriarchal authority" (2001, xiv).[17]

If anything, *Sugar Street* takes this subversion to a more pronounced level: Amina here is more independent and her movement no longer severely restricted. The third volume allows her to step outside the house more freely, though still generally for pious reasons. Given that Sayyid 'Abd al-Jawad is now old and his authority is no longer forbidding, Amina is able to visit holy shrines regularly and even pay social calls on her married daughters. After years of devoting herself to the lives of others to the point where she knows no other space than the family house, Amina is thus granted a reprieve in *Sugar Street*. Even her position within the spatial hierarchy of the house is improved, as Hafez notes. Where in the first two volumes the woman occupied the ground floor, in *Sugar Street* Amina—and other female members—are moved to the middle floor, thus creating a "quasi-parity between all members of the family" (2001, xx).

Yet, Amina remains a woman "who performs the mother's role to a degree of perfection" (Hafez 2001, 95), and who devotedly cares for the aging and ill Sayyid 'Abd al-Jawad. After the latter's death, she mourns him in a social manner appropriate for the ideal of a "proper" wife. Even in her illness, Amina maintains the image of the spiritually devout and loving mother/wife. Her brief, silent illness narrative still rehearses

17. Hafez argues that, despite Amina's outward silence, she is "the one who sets the pace and controls the space of the narrative." The critic cites the example of the "temporal arrangement of the narrative" which sees the baking room where the mother spends most of her time as integral to the unfolding of the story (2001, xiv–xvi).

traditional matriarchal values. In fact, the sick Amina becomes, if anything, more, not less, the ideal wife and mother.

Again, it is striking that Amina only falls ill after Sayyid 'Abd al-Jawad dies. She is left desolate because the "pivot of the only life" she has ever experienced has departed and, thus, she "has no further tasks to perform" in the house she has "called home for more than fifty years." To put it in her own words: "My life, which he [Sayyid 'Abd al-Jawad] once filled completely, is empty." But, for the sake of her children, she holds back her sorrow and only surrenders to it "surreptitiously" and when she is alone. She also resorts to "preparing the mercy offering" given on behalf of her husband because, as she admits, that "is all I have" (Mahfouz 1992, 209–10). Following Sayyid 'Abd al-Jawad's death, Amina is left with the care of her adult children and the nurturing of her spirituality through her frequent visits to sites of worship. In all these senses, the demise of the patriarch and the onset of her own illness only serves to strengthen—through its very absence—Amina's sense of herself as a wife and mother.

The woman, we are told, falls sick as she is preparing to visit al-Husayn shrine. As she enters the room to put on her coat, she falls and never utters a word thereafter. When the doctor arrives, he diagnoses that she suffers "from paralysis and pneumonia" (Mahfouz 1992, 304). Yet, once again, the symbolic context of the onset of her illness is unmistakable as Amina collapses on the very threshold of the domestic sphere. Firstly, her fall—right before heading to al-Husayn shrine—inevitably recalls the incident in the first volume of the trilogy that saw her being expelled from the house by her husband. Both events take place at the literal and symbolic limit where private and public spaces—and implicitly feminine and masculine spaces—meet. If it is undoubtedly true that *Sugar Street* captures the slow emergence of Egyptian women into the public sphere—including women of Amina's generation—it nonetheless depicts this passage as slow, painful, and riven by many setbacks, compromises, and failures. By depicting Amina as falling ill at the very moment that she leaves the domestic space, the novel symbolically returns her to that space forever and locks the door. In writing its own anxieties about female empowerment onto Amina's physical body, Arab patriarchy predetermines her fate and pathologizes her freedom.

Just like in *Palace Walk*, then, the third volume of the trilogy shows that leaving the domestic sphere is not without dramatic consequences. It may be that Sayyid 'Abd al-Jawad is long gone but the patriarchal system he represents continues to cast a shadow over the narrative. The paralysis that results from the fall, and which makes all movement impossible for Amina, is another symbolic symptom that a woman's place is inside the home, not beyond. To be sure, Mahfouz's trilogy captures the friction between traditional and emerging gender roles, but Amina's fall and paralysis show that he ultimately upholds core patriarchal norms in a fast-changing social milieu. If *Sugar Street* does imagine alternative lives for women than wife or mother—the journalist Sawsan Hammad is a progressive, liberal "career woman" who seems to belong in a different century from Amina—it remains the case that Amina's illness narrative ultimately domesticates, maternalizes, and sentimentalizes the female body even in its sickness.

When Amina's children try to come to terms with the idea of losing her, for example, they seek consolation in the very hegemonic patriarchal values that have consigned their mother to a maternal ideal throughout her life. It is striking that Kamal, Amina's youngest son, stresses that his mother's sickness came without warning. If there were any symptoms, he says, then his mother would not have said anything about them: "the poor woman" did not utter a single word of complaint (Mahfouz 1992, 304). In this way, Amina's life-long self-sacrifice is transformed into, and celebrated as, stoicism in the face of suffering.

The imminence of her death means that Amina's maternal importance in the life of her children takes on an ever more sentimental scope. As Kamal gazes at her "pale, silent face," he realizes that soon there would be "no one in the building to call 'Mother'." During that moment of heartache, he repeatedly exclaims: "How much she had loved him! How much she had loved all of them! How much she had loved everything in existence!" Elsewhere, he reiterates to himself: "Your mother dies after concluding a lifetime of achievement" (Mahfouz 1992, 304). When Aisha is informed of her mother's condition she proclaims: "If she lies in bed like this for a long time, life in our house will surely be unbearable" (Mahfouz 1992, 302).

In such passages, Mahfouz locates cultural and symbolic power in the figure of the mother. It is clear, from the children's reaction to Amina's illness and the prospect of her death, that it has been their mother, all along, who gave their lives meaning. Even more, the sickness affirms the spiritual and moral superiority of Amina. After all, the woman was about to embark on a visit to a holy shrine before her lapse into the silent illness. When Kamal requests that Amina postpone the visit for another day, the mother replies: "How can I have a good day if I don't visit your master al-Husayn?" (Mahfouz 1992, 303). In one sense, it is as if her final illness becomes the logical conclusion of a life of quiet, saintly devotion.

What, then, does Amina tell us about the representation of female physical illness and disability by this most renowned of Arabic writers? First of all, it is telling that Amina's illness still remains largely occluded even in the midst of a trilogy that aspires to capture every aspect of Egyptian life, culture, and society. As we have already seen in the Introduction, the character—whose subjectivity is a focal point of the trilogy as a whole—effectively disappears at the moment she becomes ill: her sickness is narrated by everyone except Amina herself. To grasp this point, we need only compare the representation of Amina's illness here with that of 'Abd al-Jawad earlier in the trilogy: the latter is afforded the space to articulate and reflect upon his own physical decline right up until the moment of his death. Even the brief narrative we are presented with regarding Amina depicts her decline as a silent, unexplained malaise rather than a corporeal experience of pain. Yet, appropriately enough for a novel that concerns a fast-changing society, *Sugar Street* marks a genuine moment of transition in the representation of the female suffering body. On the one hand, Amina's illness discloses the real and symbolic strength of the maternal and domestic bond at a moment of patriarchal crisis. On the other hand, though, the character's stoic endurance of her suffering celebrates a traditional gender function even as it attempts to show the social and political transformations underway in society. In his decision to end the novel by idealizing the silent mother figure at the moment of her death, Mahfouz affirms that—whether in illness or in health—the mother is "the unsung heroine of the family" (Hafez 2001, xix).

Hanna Mina: *Baqaya Suwar*

Published in 1975, *Baqaya Suwar* (Fragments of Memory) is a mixture of autobiography and fiction and reveals much about the social fabric of the period. The novel not only captures the dismal socio-economic conditions that the majority of Syrians faced after World War I,[18] but, more particularly, also offers an acute portrait of the lives of Syrian women during this period. In its powerful representation of the hold of patriarchy over all aspects of women's life—both in health and in illness—*Fragments of Memory* also constitutes an interesting counterpoint to *Sugar Street*.

Fragments of Memory tells the story of a poor Syrian family at the mercy of a drunken, irresponsible, and womanizing father. Despite his various plans for their survival, the family—which is made up of a mother, three daughters, and a young son—is frequently left with nothing to eat and no prospect of anything to improve its living conditions. Told from the perspective of the young son and the "narrator's older, analytic persona" (Booth 1994, 877), *Fragments of Memory* uses the story of one family to offer a general picture of an appalling period of Syrian history. Perhaps the main focus of Mina's criticism is the situation of impoverished women in a society still dominated by traditional patriarchal norms (Booth 1994, 877). In the course of this narrative, we also discover the peculiar vulnerability of the sick female body to the symbolic violence of patriarchy.

During a period of particular impoverishment, the narrator's family are forced to live for three months under a fig tree. The unhealthy environment causes most of them to become ill; the narrator (and later his sisters) contracts first an eye infection and then malaria. Yet, it is the illness of the mother that is most revealing despite, or rather because of, the fact that its precise nature remains a mystery. To put it in the narrator's words, his mother suddenly "fell subject to a malady no one knew a cure for that confined her to bed until she was at the point of death" (Mina 1993, 106). In this brief illness narrative, the impression we gather is that the mother's

18. This period saw an end to the Ottoman reign and the persistent pressure of the French mandate.

sickness is psychological in nature and caused by the enormous mental strain that her dismal life has imposed upon her.

Yet, the "twinges in her waist" (Mina 1993, 122) and the "emaciated and sallow" demeanor which makes her cheek bones stand out (Mina 1993, 110) betray the fact that this illness is not merely psychological. It has an obvious physical cause: malnutrition. After all, what finally cures the mother is drinking chicken broth: "she went to sleep and sweated" after eating the broth, the narrator recounts, "her sweat being a sign" of improvement (Mina 1993, 122). Just like the mystifying but painful sickness that afflicts the protagonist of Taymur's short story in the first section of this chapter, though, *Fragments of Memory* chooses not to explicate the physical dimension of the mother's illness and leaves its true cause in the invisible realm of psychology. If we might be tempted to attribute this reticence to the narrator alone—he is a young boy who is clearly devastated by his mother's illness—this chapter has shown that Mina's narrative is by no means exceptional in its marginalization of the female suffering body. In *Fragments of Memory*, the unwillingness or inability to name the physical illness is part of what we have seen to be a larger aesthetic strategy of rendering the ill female invisible.

The character of the mother is, revealingly, complicit in this silence. It is clear that, like Amina in *Sugar Street*, she performs the traditional gender role of submissive wife and mother almost to the end. To speak about her illness, she would have to leave behind her position as the docile, selfless caregiver and assume an entirely new identity. Yet, inevitably, this is precisely what she cannot or will not do. Even as the narrator's mother "gazed at [them] silently with an expression of wary resignation frozen in the depths of her eyes," even as "she no longer spoke," we are told that her "feeble arms" continued to "enfold" her children when they sought refuge in her bed (Mina 1993, 110–11). Despite the severity of her illness, the narrator's mother remains a gentle, selfless woman who provides "protection" for her children and who cries out in despair when her husband punished her young boy (Mina 1993, 107). She even tells them: "I am not going to die . . . I couldn't die and leave you. God will help me to get better . . . God loves the little ones. He loves them dearly so He won't allow them to remain orphans. . . . ." (Mina 1993, 112–13).

For Mina, just as for Mahfouz before him, it is clear that the mother retains a considerable measure of symbolic power, even supremacy, in her moment of greatest physical weakness. She is explicitly contrasted in the narrator's eyes with the figure of the father: whereas the mother is described as kind, caring, and generous even in extreme illness, the father comes forth as a reckless, irresponsible, and cruel figure who oppresses his wife and children. Even more, the narrator makes clear that it is his father's misdeeds that are the cause of much of his mother's humiliation and suffering. Yet, the mother withstands it all without any sign of antagonism: only her eyes "remained veiled, distressed and distracted" (Mina 1993, 110). The fact that the mother endures her illness with stoicism confirms the quiet heroism with which she has performed her domestic role throughout her life. Just as Amina's maternal role is implicitly sanctified in *Sugar Street*, so the mother in *Fragments of Memory* is also marked by her religious piety: "Heaven was looking upon us, knew about us and would help us," she proclaims to her son (Mina 1993, 121). In fact, Mina's modern depiction of female illness even harks back to the equivalent representations in Taymur's short story and al-Siba'i's novel: all three women obtain a measure of symbolic agency by turning to spirituality in the last days of their suffering.

Perhaps more than anything else in this exceptionally bleak novel, the illness of the mother serves to indict the patriarchal political and economic structures of Syrian society in the period. It becomes clear that this system not only brings about social and familial breakdown but, in her case, inflicts concrete physical harm. According to this reading, the particular failings of the narrator's father are a cipher for the failures of the patriarchal system of governance as a whole. Even though the cause of the mother's illness is never explicitly identified, one gathers that it is at least partially the result of her husband's misdeeds. For the young narrator, his mother "saw and suffered" in "her dusty resting place under the fig tree" as the family sinks further and further into debt (Mina 1993, 120). The contrast between the almost chaotic performance of the father in the public sphere and the passive, yet orderly, performance of the sick mother under the fig tree (a substitute space for the domestic house) unsettles the gender politics of power. On the one hand, the young narrator describes how his father told tales that "contained no moral: virtue and vice, the oppressor and oppressed were all the same to him. He would often make evil look good and disparage goodness. . . . ." (Mina 1993, 121). On the other hand, his mother "with her gentleness, weakness, compassion and serenity, was [his] ideal of womanhood," adding that "she was the angelic side of femininity" (Mina 1993, 127). In her physical weakness, the sick mother still appears to shift the balance of power further into the domestic sphere.

If the domestic space becomes the only true source of power, stability, and responsibility in the novel, it remains a peculiarly vulnerable one. It is no accident that, while every single member of the family suffers from a severe bout of illness, it is the mother who suffers the most. At the same time, we know that her illness is itself the physical sign of the degradation of the maternal sphere by the indifference, inequalities, and injustices of the masculine world of work. To this extent, it is incredibly poignant that the sole domestic refuge left to the family remains, at the same time, one which is utterly exposed to the outside world: the fig tree. When the family moves into this surrogate domestic space, of course, the mother immediately succumbs to her illness. The narrator himself elaborates on the fear that took hold of his mother when she had to live "under an open sky," and the utter mortification she felt at being subjected to the gaze of strangers. In this sense, the mother's illness also becomes a symptom of the breakdown of social order as the domestic sphere is effectively laid bare to all.

In a similar way to *Sugar Street*, then, *Fragments of Memory* seems to point (historically, politically, and aesthetically) in two directions at once. It is simultaneously revolutionary and conservative. It bemoans the political and economic failings of traditional, patriarchal society and celebrates the stereotype of domestic womanhood that society most reveres. It lambasts the physical injury that Syrian society of the period inflicts upon its most vulnerable members but affirms the quiet fortitude and resilience of the victims themselves. For Mina, then, we might go so far as to say that the female suffering body constitutes both the death throes of the old patriarchal order and its last gasp: the sick mother performs her traditional domestic role to the end—quietly, submissively, and piously—even as everyone else crumbles around her.

Three Patterns of Representation

In the course of this chapter, we have observed three patterns emerge in the representation of female physical illness and disability: the "fallen" woman, the embodiment of the nation in crisis, and the ideal mother/wife. This concluding section will seek to critically reassess these three distinct tropes one by one, to compare them and to bring them into dialogue with each other.

Firstly, it is striking that Taymur's "Wa Usdila al-Sitar" and al-Siba'i's *Nahnu la Nazra'u al-Shawk* portray the "fallen" ill female either as single or widowed, that is to say, as a woman who has failed to secure a permanent position in the domestic sphere. It is also the case that her sickness generally emerges at the end of a life of sin (usually sexual promiscuity) as a symbolic punishment for her actions and/or an opportunity to seek redemption albeit through extreme suffering. Both texts depict their respective protagonists reproaching themselves for their actions and rededicating themselves to a life of virtue, domesticity, and piety. Yet, even so, the illness has no cure: the only hope of relief for the female character lies in the promise of a spiritual afterlife. From a symptom of spiritual punishment, bodily pain becomes (in a deeply problematic fashion) the road to purification and redemption in the next world. In this way, both Taymur and al-Siba'i's portrayals of the physically sick woman transform an illness narrative into a moral rite of passage or even a religious mission.

It is also clear that the transformation of illness into a narrative of transgression and redemption—both by the author and the female narrators themselves—militates against any socially or politically progressive dimension the texts may possess. As we have seen, the act of narrating their own life—and of reconstructing an identity shattered by deviance—becomes a means for the ill female narrators to symbolically reintegrate themselves into the social order. However, it is paradoxically this act of symbolic narration that undercuts the overall attempt of the texts—particularly in al-Siba'i's novel—to highlight and criticize the debased status of women in society at the time. The emphasis on representing the ill female body within a framework of notions of sin and redemption serves to reinforce traditional discourses regarding the performance of womanhood, even in states of illness. In Bakhtinian terms, a male-oriented "monologic" voice and a largely "singular" social and ideological language permeates the voice of both female protagonists (1981, 269–75).

Secondly, we have explored attempts to render the sick/disabled female a symbolic or metaphoric embodiment of the state of the nation. In both Kanafani's *Rijal fi al-Shams* (Men in the Sun) and Qasim's *Abna' al-Qal'a*, we saw how female disability becomes a marker of the scarred state of the nation, specifically Palestine. It is the disabled female body, more than any other, which embodies the pain, alienation, and injuries of the nation. Herein, the loss of limbs does not merely signify an inability to perform a domestic role but also a larger national malaise or immobility. The disabled woman's failure to have children also strips her of all maternal qualities, even or especially the biopolitical maternal role of reproducing the nation. This means that she no longer qualifies for the role of "symbol of maternal self-sacrifice or . . . the nation's fierce 'virginal' pride" in the "national family drama" which is regarded as an emblematic feature of colonial and postcolonial narratives (Boehmer 2005, 28–29). Nevertheless, despite, or because of, the social isolation that accompanies the character's disability, the ill female begins to embody an alternative symbolic space of nationhood. For both Kanafani and Qasim, the disabled female body incarnates a place of refuge—a mother for the motherless, a home for the homeless.

The illness narratives in both texts also offer an ironic counterpoint to prevailing political rhetoric, formations, and ideology. To return to the figure of Shafiqa, we saw how her illness narrative captures the growing disenchantment with the ideological strategy of certain Arab states to present a collective and unified Arab identity in the face of a "foreign" enemy. By transforming Shafiqa's wounded body into a symbol of the nation, and by showing how she is compelled to endure her pain in total isolation, the illness narrative subverts the whole notion of a collective, monolithic, and mutually supportive Arab body. Perhaps more poignantly still, her indifferent, isolated, and immobile fate foreshadows the fate of the men in the text. What, ultimately, is the difference between the disabled woman in the house and the miserable men in the sun? In her lonely illness, Shafiqa foretells the fate of Palestine itself amidst the disintegration of the Pan-Arab ideal.

Finally, we have seen that Arab male literature during this period also portrays the ill female as a passive, saintly, and traditional mother figure. She may endure her suffering in the silence of her room/world but her sickness enriches the maternal bonds that exist between mother and child and subtly subvert patriarchal authority. For Mahfouz and Mina, the sick mother exists solely within the domestic domain and her authority derives from her morality and spirituality. In Mina's work, in particular, the sanctification of the sick mother figure also stands in stark contrast to the debasement of traditional patriarchal values: the mother's goodness is juxtaposed with the reckless and almost evil actions of the father. This affirmation of the matriarch fills the gap left behind by an exhausted or dying patriarch. In *al-Sukkariya* (Sugar Street), Amina falls sick after her husband passes away.

Although the sick mother in both novels remains a silent, voiceless woman, her representation takes on more complex significance than in the works discussed earlier. After all, the mother in these novels—in both sickness and health—is pivotal to the narrative: Amina is, as Hafez argues, "not only the hub of the family," but the one who "controls the space of the narrative" (2001, xiv). For Hafez, her presence, albeit implicitly, bespeaks of the "dwindling of patriarchy in Egypt's painful path to modernity" (2001, xiv). In *Baqaya Suwar* (Fragments of Memory), too, the whole narrative account of the mother's sickness, the legitimacy she gains in the eyes of her children—even in her deteriorating health—and the blame that is repeatedly conferred upon the patriarch for their predicament, reflects the rise of matriarchal authority at the expense of the law of the father.

What, to bring this chapter to a close, do all three tropes for the female suffering body—the moral, national, and the domestic—have in common? It is crucial to underscore that—for all the differences between and within them—each serves to effectively render the ill body silent and invisible. It is clear that—whether older or more contemporary, whether traditional and nostalgic or modern and progressive—Arab male writing still attaches a certain stigma to female illness and disability throughout this period. Female illness and disability signals the end of femininity and, more importantly, feminine sexuality, in the eyes of all the writers under discussion. First, all the works analyzed present the physically sick female as a spinster, a widow, a divorcee, or a child-like character. In each text, the woman falls ill at a time when all hopes of marriage dissipate (Taymur, al-Siba'i, and Qasim), or when her husband no longer performs his traditional patriarchal role toward her or her children, or when the latter has simply died (Mina and Mahfouz). When a male protagonist does acknowledge the visibility of the ill female body—like Marwan's father's decision to marry the disabled Shafiqa in *Men in the Sun*—it is only because he has, in some real or symbolic sense, relinquished his patriarchal or masculine role. In the case of Marwan's father, recall, he is a desperate man who abandons the family home to obtain security and comfort in his old age.

Such textual strategies of marginalizing the suffering woman play out in various ways, both literal and metaphorical. It is striking, for example, that she is quite literally consigned to the periphery of the house. After all, the anonymous protagonist in Taymur's short story suffers her illness in the isolation of her room; Shafiqa's house is located on the edges of the town; the mother in Mina's narrative never utters a word; Amina lives her physical pain within the obliviousness of her room. If the ill body is left in obscurity, the precise nature of its illness is also occluded: it is either not specified at all (Taymur and Mina) or it is chronic and incurable. In both cases, the corporeal body literally disappears.

For the majority of the writers under discussion, however, the most important symptom of this marginalization of the corporeal body is its metaphorical transformation into a social or political body. It is only by being put into discourse that the ill woman becomes visible. By filling the textual vacuum where the corporeal reality of the ill body should be with discourse, Arab male writing seeks to exculpate itself (whether religiously or politically) from its failure to represent that physical body: stigmatism becomes symbolism. If it seeks to turn female physical illness and disability into something other than itself, we have also seen that Arab male writing still cannot ignore the stubborn, irreducible materiality of that body. In this sense, the literature examined in this chapter is marked by competing and irreconcilable desires and anxieties: it simultaneously seeks to render female illness and disability visible and invisible, silent and eloquent, a privileged sign of the body politic to be championed and a failed image of ideal womanhood to be shut away forever.

Perhaps another powerful anxiety at work in the (non-)representation of the ill female body in these texts is, of course, a traditional patriarchal fear in an epoch of increasing female empowerment. It is possible to argue that, in many of the works under discussion in this chapter, female physical illness and disability becomes the inverse sign of female social and political mobilization. As we saw in the case of Taymur's narrative, illness becomes a kind of pathologized punishment for transgressive behavior within the public sphere. Similarly, al-Siba'i's pain-wracked protagonist considers herself fortunate because fate has removed her from her "fallen" public sphere and placed her in the domestic world of her employers. In a similar vein, we might speculate that even the precise nature of Shafiqa and Fawziya's disabilities is highly symbolic: both lose physical mobility and with it the freedom to move beyond the private sphere.

If Arab male writers have an interest in the female suffering body, then, we might be tempted to note that they always see it through the lens of another body in pain: the increasingly fragile, vulnerable, and traumatized *male* body.[19] In other words, the female suffering body suffers from a

19. In her study of the modern Egyptian novel, for example, Hilary Kilpatrick identifies four categories of writers based on their perception and representation of women: (1) writers who were unconcerned with the plight of women and who, instead, focused on other socio-political problems; (2) writers who depicted a woman's role in society but whose work remained enmeshed in traditional views of womanhood; (3) writers who perceived women as starkly different from men and hence "objects of desire"; and (4) writers who sought to explicitly explore the status of women in society and were, in a sense, "social reformers" (1974, 172–78). To apply Kilpatrick's taxonomy to the authors and works under consideration in this chapter, we might argue that Taymur belongs in the first category: his story holds tight to a traditional view of womanhood. Although still traditional, al-Siba'i's account manifests greater sensitivity in its attempt to highlight the plight of his heroine. On the other hand, both Kanafani and Qasim's female illness narratives are largely unconcerned with gender dynamics and locate their female protagonists against the backdrop of larger national political ideologies. Finally, Mahfouz and Mina's illness narratives reveal the "social reform" stance toward women's place and role in society but ultimately adopt a more traditional position in relation to their female characters.

taboo within the larger taboo that afflicts the female body more generally: she is a problem within the larger problem of female sexuality that haunts the Arab male psyche.[20]

In conclusion, then, we must return to the absence with which we began this chapter. It is not enough to say that the physically ill/disabled female body is largely absent from Arab male writing between 1950 to 2000 because *even when it is present* it is rendered absent. The ill woman lacks an individual body, affect, subjectivity, or consciousness. Quite simply, the female protagonist's voice becomes little more than the subject of an act of patriarchal and ideological ventriloquism: the words she speaks are not her own. Even or especially when the ill woman speaks, she is rendered silent. To this extent, the female suffering body can perhaps be seen as an example of what Judith Butler calls the necessary "outside" of the normalized, healthy body: "It will be as important to think about how and to what end bodies are constructed as it will be to think about how and to what end bodies are not constructed and, further, to ask after how bodies which fail to materialize provide the necessary 'outside,' if not the necessary support, for the bodies which, in materializing the norm, qualify as bodies that matter" (1993, 16).

If female physical illness and disability is "outside" Arab male writing of the period, though, it is not because it is denied discursive construction but rather because it is so totally dominated by the prevailing symbolic discourses: the female suffering body is all the more thoroughly excluded

20. Perhaps one might argue that the representation of female sickness in Western literature and culture has also captured this gendered ambivalence. It has also told a similar story of stigma. However, one key difference in the nature of the discourse of the stigmatized approach to female illness is that Western representations of female illness articulate the workings of this stigma and give room for this stigmatized self to express the injustices directed at her. Furthermore, the period after World War II witnessed a dramatic change in the understanding of illness in general and female illness in particular, with the latter becoming part and parcel of modern and postmodern productions, altering the stigmatized modes through which female illness was represented. This, however, is not the case in Arabic literature and culture, particularly during the period emphasized in this chapter.

by being included in a discourse which is not its own. By turning that body inside out, so to speak, Arab male writing explodes its interiority and occludes the subjective phenomenological experience of suffering, illness, and sickness. They represent what Jeanne Kammer, in her discussion of the art of silence, has called an "acknowledgement of the void, a falling-back in the face of chaos, nothing," rather than a "determination to enter that darkness, to use it, to illuminate it with individual presence" (1979, 158). In the remainder of this book, we will turn to those Arab writers—both male and female—who do seek to enter the darkness of female physical illness and disability and to illuminate it with the individual presence of countless suffering women.

MEDIATING VOICES

Illness and Disability in Female Writing, 1950–2000

In this chapter, we turn to the representation of female physical illness and disability in Arab women's writing. It is with women's writing—even more than its male equivalent—that the singular absence of the female suffering body is most strongly and poignantly felt. Yet, as we will see, it is arguably even more difficult to find representations of female illness and disability in women's writing than it is in writing by men. For Arab male writers like Kanafani and Mahfouz, it is possible to argue that the ill female body *is* present—albeit in a spectral, marginal, and occluded form. In the work of their female counterparts, however, this body is almost totally absent, removed, abjected.

To be sure, it is hardly surprising that the physical body in pain has no place in Arab women's writing of the period, given the social, cultural, and political transformations that were underway from the 1950s onward. After all, the female physical body in general (particularly the sexualized body) was repeatedly pushed outside the sphere of female narratives so that writers could underscore less transgressive aspects of women's lives and existence: the submissive, the domestic, the maternal. For many women writers, in other words, the attitude toward the sick female body was just as reductive as that of their male equivalents: female physical illness and disability are stigmatized for their failure to live up to a normative idea of womanhood shared by both men and many women alike. In representing female physical illness/disability, women writers ultimately "reproduce[d] not only the world view inherent in the predominantly masculine discourse, but also adopt[ed] its version of the passive, docile, selfless female" (Hafez 1995, 161).

This chapter will focus on the representation of female physical illness and disability in selected works of Arab women writers from 1950 to 2000. It will seek, like the previous chapter, to decipher the various semiotic, socio-cultural, and political codes that have encrypted the female suffering body in Arabic literature in this period. The argument will explore the extent to which Arab women's writing perpetuates, deepens, and resists the traditional patriarchal idea of what it means to be female and physically sick. If women writers internalize and reproduce patriarchal representations of female physical illness/disability, however, we will also see that they struggle to overcome this discursive stranglehold and give voice to the female body in pain. In Arab women's writing, the female suffering body—so long silenced—begins, however haltingly, to speak.

Barren Lives/Disrupted Womanhood

In Arab health discourses, two forms of female physical illness/disability predominate: infertility and blindness. It is not surprising, then, to find that these forms also play a major role in literary representations of the ill/disabled woman. For many writers "female sickness" is located almost exclusively in either the eyes or the womb. Yet, in very few instances—particularly in works by women writers—do infertility and blindness become more than simply forms of physical illness or disability: they are employed as organizing metaphors for women's embodiment, gender, and social identity. In this section, we will examine the work of two women writers of the 1950s and 1960s who represented the ill and disabled woman both literally and symbolically: Syrian Colette Khoury and Huyam Nuwaylati.

Huyam Nuwaylati: *Fi al-Layl*[1]

In Nuwaylati's first novel *Fi al-Layl* (In the Night, 1959), for example, we encounter perhaps the only novel published in the 1950s by an Arab

1. Little is known about the Syrian writer Nuwaylati and her works except what is provided on the back cover of her first novel *Fi al-Layl*. Her name and publications are absent

woman writer to focus on the representation of a female physical disability: blindness. Unfortunately, the novel is out of print and now difficult to find, but it remains a crucial and neglected contribution to the discourse of female sickness/disability during the period. For Malti-Douglas, blind women were not "completely absent in historical and some limited literary sources" from the Arab and Islamic tradition, but they were still "textually rare and do not become foci or topoi" (1991, 125). This novel is an exception to the rule.

Written largely in the form of an autobiography, *Fi al-Layl* concerns an unnamed female student who has a relationship with her music instructor. The instructor attempts to seduce the student both emotionally and sexually, but the latter rejects him (even though she loves him). As revenge, the instructor ensures she fails her music exam and destroys her hope of a career in that field. Following a nightmare, the student wakes up to find that she has become blind. She goes on to settle in Egypt and becomes a famous flute player. At this point in the narrative, she meets her music instructor's son, befriends him, and then gives him a copy of an autobiography she has written to pass on to his father. This autobiography—a book composed by a blind woman—becomes the basis of the narrative itself.

It is immediately striking, of course, that female blindness in *Fi al-Layl* is not a physical handicap the protagonist is born with. Nor is it the result of an accident. Rather, its sudden onset seems to have no clinical cause whatsoever. In the text, the protagonist simply declares that she became blind and, revealingly, never seeks a clinical diagnosis of her condition. Clearly, it is her emotional trauma that is the root cause of her blindness,

---

from literary reference books and studies both on Arabic literature and women's writings. Except for a short reference to her novel *Fi al-Layl*, in Buthayna Sha'aban's book *Mi'at 'Am min al-Riwaya al-Nisa'iya al-'Arabiyya*, Nuwaylati's name does not find a place in most literary studies. Yet, as Sha'aban notes, from her very few publications one gathers that she had been a writer of some standing. She published a biography of the Muslim scholar al-Ghazali, while her collection of prose *Ayyami* (My Days) was introduced by Egyptian critic and writer Taha Husayn. She also published a novel entitled *Washm 'ala al-Hawa'* (A Tattoo in the Air) and a collection of poetry entitled *Kayfa Tumahhi al-Ab'ad* (How to Shorten the Distance; 1999, 90).

and the woman invokes her loss of sight as a means of articulating the desolation she feels after the acrimonious collapse of her relationship with her tutor.

During her illness narrative, the protagonist's focus is always upon her emotional rather than physical loss. Thus, blindness becomes a kind of pathological metaphor for the protagonist's melancholic state upon losing the man she loved. Once again, it is crucial to note the precise moment when illness strikes the victim: the blindness occurs after she realizes that her love affair is doomed. She cries herself to sleep then wakes to the sound of herself screaming, "I have lost him . . . lost him forever," and to find that a "heavy mist . . . was preventing me from seeing. . . ." Later, she adds: "And with that my lids closed to [his] presence" and "eternal darkness united me with the one I love" (Nuwaylati 1959, 152).

Rather than an experience of physical deprivation, the protagonist's loss of sight actually becomes a psychological comfort zone that makes her feel "protected from cruel loneliness" and even "transported to a new world" (Nuwaylati 1959, 122–23). It also marks her withdrawal into an internal world distant from any external stimuli that might interfere with her musical talents. In short, blindness symbolically enables the protagonist to shut out the world and to retreat into a self-created space of musical harmony.

Not only is the process of becoming blind presented in sentimental, even melodramatic terms, but the condition of blindness itself is also romanticized. When the son of her instructor observes the protagonist performing on stage, years after the onset of her condition, his descriptions of her are striking: the blind musician, as everyone identified her, covered her eyes with dark sunglasses, reacted to the applause of the audience with "dignity and kindness," and took on a special, ethereal beauty when she began to play her flute. Remote and mysterious, she declined all invitations and left the theatre immediately after her performance ended (Nuwaylati 1959, 20–21). For the instructor's son, watching the flute player is akin to gazing at a spectral entity who barely seems to exist when she is off stage. In a sense, she embodies what Laura Mulvey, in her classic work on visual pleasure and narrative cinema, calls "to-be-looked-at-ness" (1977, 412–28).

Despite the acclaim the protagonist enjoys, her blindness still isolates her from the world of others. It also places her within a classical literary tradition which, according to Malti-Douglas, saw "women and the blind . . . relegated to the same mental universe: one of physicality, relative physical imperfection and social marginality" (1991, 124). As Malti-Douglas further notes, this tradition saw the two figures occupying a similar "syntagmatic" relationship to the extent that discussions of women and the blind were always placed at the end of any literary collection. This association between blindness and femininity in the classic tradition is perpetuated, indeed deepened, in modern Arabic literature, albeit with one significant difference.[2] In Nuwaylati's novel, of course, the protagonist finds herself doubly marginalized: both blind *and* a woman.

Yet, like the male writers we discussed in chapter 1, Nuwaylati cannot help but transform the female musician's physical disability into a metaphor. It is ultimately nothing more than the physical symptom of her enduring romantic devotion to her teacher. By symbolically "choosing" darkness and the memory of her beloved over any new experience of the world, the flautist performs the ultimate gesture of love and sacrifice. In her romanticization of the female suffering body, Nuwaylati carries on the sentimental patriarchal tradition found also in the works of romantic male writers such as Taymur and al-Siba'i.

For Nuwaylati, however, the protagonist's blindness also has a more complex textual purpose. It is intriguing that she is not the only "blind" character in the novel: her male teacher fails to recognize her talent as a student or to acknowledge her later fame as an accomplished musician. Accordingly, female physical blindness becomes symptomatic of a prior male gendered and social blindness: the patriarchal teacher's own failings are displaced (in a gesture that the novel both criticizes and is, to some extent, complicit with) onto the body of his student. By becoming

2. For example in Ghada al-Samman's short story "Ghajariya Bila Marfa'" (Street Walker) the blind man is the "alter-ego" of the protagonist. Also, Andrée Chedid's novel *Le Sommeil délivré* (From Sleep Unbound) draws parallels between a blind man and the heroine, while in Assia Djebar's novel *L'amour, la Fantasia* (Fantasia: An Algerian Cavalcade), a veiled female is compared to a blind individual (See Malti-Douglas 1991, 122–23).

a distinguished musician herself, the protagonist challenges her music instructor's "blind" verdict of her abilities and begins—if not to see with her own eyes—to speak in her own voice. When she slowly gains mastery over music, and independence from the persecutor of her talents, her narrative voice begins to emerge. It is no coincidence here that, while the first half of the novel is told from the point of view of the musician's son, the second half is focalized by the protagonist herself. The hinge moment between the two parts of the text is the musical performance—witnessed by her teacher's son—which is the final validation of her talent. In a larger sense, *Fi al-Layl* is itself something of a hinge text, delicately balanced between tradition and modernity, between patriarchy and social reform, between a woman who chooses not to see and a woman who (finally) learns how to speak.

Colette Khoury: *Layla Wahida*

Published in 1961, *Layla Wahida* (One Night) created controversy upon its first appearance due to the novel's sympathetic approach to the taboo subject of adultery.[3] To be sure, Khoury's novel is remarkably modern in tone, theme, and social attitudes for its time. It depicts female adultery not simply as something to be stigmatized but as a source of increasing power, agency, and self-awareness for women. If Khoury's work often represents women as finding strength in themselves, however, the overarching mood of this novel is despair. In *Layla Wahida*, the source of this despair is once again the female suffering body and, in particular, the infertile body.

It is the story of Rasha, a married infertile woman who travels to Paris to find treatment for her presumed "illness" that Khoury's novel recounts. On the train taking her from Marseilles to Paris, where she is to visit a famous gynecologist, Rasha meets the half-Syrian, half-French Kameel. The two fall in love at first sight and have a passionate one-night affair. Despite the fact that the brief relationship gives Rasha emotional and sexual fulfillment, she is plagued by guilt and decides to write a letter confessing all to her husband. This letter forms the bulk of the narrative.

3. Throughout the analysis I will quote from the subsequent edition (1970 imprint).

Following the letter's completion, Rasha meets the French gynecologist only to discover that she has been misled by her Syrian doctors: it is her husband who is infertile and she is able to have children after all. In the final pages of the book, Rasha roams the streets of Paris pondering what to do with her life but, tragically, she is struck by a car and the novel ends with her in the ambulance predicting her imminent death.

As we have just seen, *Layla Wahida* principally focuses on Rasha's unhappy marriage and her (all too brief) journey to self-discovery and new love, but the novel is also a condensed but ambiguous and multi-layered illness narrative. It is not merely an account of one woman's experience of her own presumed "sickness" but of the extent to which that experience is mediated through social discourse about female infertility within Arab culture. To this extent, Rasha's illness/infertility highlights a particular cultural phenomenon identified by Inhorn whereby male infertility is attributed to a failure in the woman's body. In her research on female infertility, masculinity, and sexuality in the Middle East, Inhorn argues that "not only are women typically blamed for the reproductive failing, but they must bear the burden of overcoming it . . ." (1994, 3). This typically means that women are also charged with the responsibility of seeking treatment for their husbands' infertility, "a form of asymmetrical gendered embodiment that leaves men physically unscathed" (2012, 14).

What is made visible in Rasha's indirect illness narrative is thus not her physical body but rather her social body whose role and place is determined by gender norms. For Rasha, infertility constitutes less a physical defect than a failure to live up to her prescribed role in society: it is a failure of the will.[4] If this moral failure expresses itself physically, it is only because it has been medicalized: a social deficit is once again symbolically confirmed in a set of physiological symptoms. In this sense, female physical illness in *Layla Wahida* is once again a metaphor for a peculiarly male or patriarchal set of anxieties about the sickness of the social or political body.

4. For a study on female infertility and the failure of will see Margarete J. Sandelowski (1990).

To be sure, Rasha is a more socially and physically mobile female suffering body than any we have encountered so far—much of the narrative is based on the journey motif—but once again her actual physical condition goes largely unexplored. Throughout the narrative, Rasha is more concerned about the state of her marriage, the impact of her traditional upbringing, and her general sense of restlessness and unfulfillment than with her physical problem. Rather, the protagonist's infertility is, if anything, an excuse to travel in the hope of finding temporary respite from her life in Damascus. For Rasha, infertility is merely a physical symptom of a more general social failure to do anything normatively deemed to be "worthwhile" with her life: it is revealing that her desire to become a mother springs less from a personal wish or family pressure than from a desire to be "useful." In Diana Tietjens Meyers's study of motherhood and agency, we see that Rasha's predicament speaks to a more general social problem for women: "[T]he family does not exist in isolation from other social systems" and "women's motherhood decisions have implications for their [self] aspirations" (2001, 735–36).

Perhaps we might go so far as to say that Rasha's desire to have children is not merely due to the pressure exerted by social norms of gender, health, and illness but of the *internalization* of those norms into existential and ontological conditions. When she reminds her husband of the dismal course of their life together, for instance, she admits that she saw motherhood as the last hope that would salvage her meaningless existence. She desperately wanted to conceive because she was in need of "giving . . . to feel that I was alive . . . to prove to myself that I was alive." In Rasha's narrative, childbirth seems to be the only thing that will give her life and her death significance: her body is like a "volcano that was afraid to die before it erupts" (Khoury 1970, 26).

If Rasha's infertility is described as an illness both by herself and the doctors who are treating her, the narrative more generally makes clear that its root cause is social and ontological. It is strangely appropriate that Rasha never refers to the exact physical nature of her illness (she calls it the "sickness" or the "problem") because this is a novel in which physical illness is abstract, disembodied, and socially determined. At the same time, Rasha's inability to live up to what is expected of her as a woman means that not merely her physical illness but her whole sense of identity become socially occluded. For Khoury's protagonist, the novel becomes an act of social and physical rebellion against the society that renders her and her body redundant.

In Khoury's novel—just as in that of Nuwaylati—the female protagonist's act of self-assertion takes narrative form: the letter that Rasha composes for her husband to read. It is clear that her textual rebellion against social invisibility remains an incomplete project, however, both on the level of narrative structure and content. As we have seen, Rasha's physical and personal journey toward a new life (in an uncanny echo of the journey in *Men in the Sun*) ends in death. For Rasha, the encounter with Kameel offers her a glimpse of a new, erotic, and non-instrumental relationship to her body: "For the first time in my life I understood the value of my body . . . for the first time I understood that this body is not a tool . . ." (Khoury 1970, 191). Yet, even when the novel seems to point toward a new kind of body politics, it remains mired in the old, patriarchal one. When Rasha reviews her life as a middle class woman within a male-dominated society, it is clear that she still evaluates that life according to the patriarchal ideals of womanhood that have rendered her so thoroughly marginalized. She does not speak in her own voice so much as lip-sync what Meyers would call "the ominous baritone of patriarchy" (2001, 739). The "narrative closure" brings about what Molly Hite, in a wider study of women's narratives, terms "an enclosure" which withholds social power from the protagonist of *Layla Wahida* (1989, 4–11). In Khoury's narrative—as in so many by her male predecessors—it seems that the only freedom women can obtain from the stigma of illness and disability is death.

Sick Mothers/Rebellious Daughters

In the 1980s and 1990s, Arab women's writing on female physical illness returns to a trope with which we are already familiar: the sick mother. It is a repetition with a difference, however, because whereas writers like Mahfouz and Mina use the sick mother to affirm patriarchal ideals, modern women writers take a more complex and variegated stance toward this classic figure. This section will examine the representation of the female suffering body in Lebanese Hanan al-Shaykh's *Faras al-Shaytan*, Iraqi Alia

Mamdouh's *Habbat al-Naftaleen*, and Egyptian Salwa Bakr's *al-'Araba al-Dhahabiya la Tas'ad ila al-Sama'*. What role does female physical illness and disability—particularly embodied in the figure of the sick mother—play in a set of narratives typified by what Hafez calls a "sophisticated discourse of self-realization" (1995, 170)?

Hanan al-Shaykh: *Faras al-Shaytan*

In al-Shaykh's second novel, *Faras al-Shaytan* (Satan's She-Horse, 1975)—which is not as widely read as her other works—the celebrated contemporary Arab novelist provides us with one of the earliest representations of the trope of the sick mother in women's writings. Al-Shaykh tells the story of a young Lebanese Shi'ite Muslim woman, Sara, who is raised by a strict religious father. The novel goes on to chronicle Sara's marital relationship, her life in an unidentified desert region, and her encounter in that region with women from a harem. For al-Shaykh, Sara's life and passage between traditional and marginal social structures becomes an opportunity to interrogate the construction of Arab society from the bottom up, and the text stands as a stinging indictment of patriarchy. In the midst of this narrative, we encounter Sara's sick mother.

It is apparent that the novel's very brief reference to the illness of Sara's mother is not intended to uncover the impact of pain upon female bodies and selves. Again, the physical body is merely the site on which patriarchal discourses are inscribed. Yet, al-Shaykh's text takes a very different stance than that of Khoury toward the law of the father: the sick mother reveals the callousness of patriarchal authority and its failure to live up to its role as protector of the domestic space. In Sara's opinion, for example, the death of her mother is wholly the result of her father's indifference toward his ailing wife.

According to her grandmother—who witnesses the death of Sara's mother firsthand—the woman experienced "terrible pain" for days as she lay "burning" with fever and whimpering endlessly. Yet, Sara's father refused to fetch a doctor for his wife claiming: "Allah is the doctor" (al-Shaykh 1975, 59). When he finally relented, it was too late and the mother had already passed away. By dwelling on the last moments of the mother's suffering, and juxtaposing it with the image of the father absorbed in fervent prayer, al-Shaykh transforms the sick woman into an iconic victim of patriarchy.[5] In recalling her mother's illness, Sara herself passionately exclaims: "This is not right! This is madness!" (al-Shaykh 1975, 59).

In *Faras al-Shaytan*, though, it is also telling that the sick mother never speaks in her own voice. She dies before Sara is old enough to truly be conscious of her presence and influence. Thus, al-Shaykh marks a discontinuity between mother and daughter and, more generally, between two very different experiences of patriarchy:[6] the sick and dying mother here exemplifies the repression from which the daughter wishes to escape. By blaming her father for her mother's death, Sara is also deploring his treatment of his child: Sara, too, has had to bear the burden of his religious fanaticism. If the sick mother comes to represent the universal figure of the female victim of male oppression, though, it is arguably at the cost of, once again, occluding the particularity of the mother herself. The relation to the mother is, as Adrienne Rich argues in another context, almost "minimized and trivialized in the annals of patriarchy" (1976, 236). In her exclusive tendency to see her mother through the lens of an oppressive patriarchy, Sara ironically colludes in her father's marginalization of the ill woman.

Alia Mamdouh: *Habbat al-Naftaleen*

With Mamdouh's *Habbat al-Naftaleen* (Mothballs), however, a more complex and radical representation of the sick mother figure begins to be constructed. Mamdouh's second novel is set in Iraq in the 1950s and grapples with the question of freedom in family relations. Published in 1986, the novel offers a miniature portrait of the city of Baghdad and the dynamics of gendered relations through an intimate picture of one poor family occupying the Baghdadi neighborhood of al-A'dhamiyya. The story unfolds through the eyes of nine-year-old Huda, the youngest member of the family whose life story forms the locus of the narrative.

5. For a study of sick mothers and their deaths see Judith Kegan Gardiner (1978).

6. Dorothy Dinnerstein discusses in detail the idea of continuity and connection to the mother generally (1976).

In its account of Huda's relationship with her own sick mother, Iqbal, Mamdouh's novel opens a new phase in the representation of female physical illness.

It begins by tackling head-on the prevailing discourse of stigma that has attached itself to female physical illness in the Arab world. At the heart of the story of Huda's mother is a physical illness that leaves both her and her family in disgrace: tuberculosis. For Huda, Iqbal's illness generates a sense of shame at the latter's invisible suffering body together with an unconscious resentment at her mother's submissiveness. In fact, the novel opens with a vivid description of the rhetoric of stigma and shame to which Arab patriarchy subjects the ill female body.

Shuttling between the first, second, and third person, Huda begins her narrative by imagining that her cruel father is "driving a truck" while her mother "is sitting in the back, monopolizing the silence and illness" (Mamdouh 1996, 1). Huda's young mind already begins to chart out an oppressive, gendered division within her family and particularly between her mother and father. Her sense of division is more heightened because Iqbal suffers a chronic physical ailment that leaves her subject to daily humiliation. When Huda's father repeatedly barges into the house, filling the domestic space with what Huda describes as "an evil spirit," her mother simply "vanished out of his way" (Mamdouh 1996, 4). The young girl observes that her mother "took all her guidance" from her husband and "never dared reject his bidding." She "sullied no one with her voice" and responded to the bullying around her "with a brief nod of her head." In short, Iqbal kept her "dark curtain of secrecy around her narrow domain" (Mamdouh 1996, 5).

The miserable existence of Huda's mother—filled with daily silent rituals—exposes the total alienation of the female suffering body from the world that surrounds her. Only the symptoms of her illness reverberate through the house, striking fear into her own children, instigating a series of curses from her sister-in-law, and prayers from her mother-in-law. For Huda, Iqbal's "sharp coughing travelled through walls and windows," to the point where she and her brother Adil felt so "encircled" by it that they were forced to seek refuge in their grandmother's room. In the brief moments of respite from pain, Huda's mother is still unable to escape her abject condition: when she laughed "she asked God's protection from Satan" and her "facial features became tense as she remembered that laughter is a sort of sin" (Mamdouh 1996, 5).

To Huda and her brother, Iqbal's illness remains something they "did not know" about precisely because they "did not want to know" and the elders "did not want [them] to know" (Mamdouh 1996, 5). It is once again apparent that the female suffering body triggers what Thomas J. Scheft calls "an endless chain reaction of unacknowledged shame" that moves "both within persons and between them . . ." (2000, 90). As we have seen in other texts, the ill woman seems to physically disappear: she can be traced only in the empty spaces she leaves behind and the adverse reactions of her family. Perhaps most dramatically, Iqbal's illness is measured through its psychological impact upon Huda herself: she is clearly a traumatized, fractured narrator, split between the fatal knowledge that something is desperately wrong with her mother and the consolatory desire to repress that knowledge. The narrative index of her traumatized subjectivity is that Huda continually refers to herself in the second and the third person rather than the first. In this respect, she exemplifies what Christopher Bollas calls the "psychic confusion" generated by the attempt to narrate the traumatic event. Bollas argues that "psychic confusion is part of the full effect of trauma because, unable to narrate the event in the first place, the person now re-experiences isolation, this time brought on by the loneliness of mental confusion" (1993, 67).

The young girl's trauma is sharpened in her daily interactions with the outside world because the public sphere transfers the shame of Huda's mother's illness onto Huda herself. At the women's *hammam* (public bath), one female neighbor wonders whether anyone would ever consider marrying Huda because "she's weak and pale" and seems to have "her mother's illness" (Mamdouh 1996, 23). Indeed, the women even begin to examine the girl for symptoms of Iqbal's disease. For Huda's friend Mahmoud, too, mother and daughter are equally contaminated. When Huda tries to tell him that her mother's "chest is pierced with holes like a sieve" and that "maybe everybody's chest has holes," Mahmoud insists on the singularity of Iqbal's illness and even admits he has been warned against playing with Huda herself: "'Don't play with Huda—she'll infect you'." In response, Huda can only mentally recite the catechism: "Infection, tuberculosis, isolation" (Mamdouh 1996, 24).

For Huda, such experiences of social abjection once again highlight the precarious social position occupied by the female suffering body and, indeed, by the female body more generally under patriarchy. At her own early age, she is already being warned that her mother's illness will minimize her chances of marriage later in life. Quite simply, Iqbal's illness de-feminizes Huda by proxy: the daughter will not be able to perform the proper role earmarked for her by society. In her encounter with Mahmoud, Huda also begins to glimpse the uneven distribution of physical and social power between male and female bodies: "I was smaller than he. I was female and he was male . . . He was able to do many things . . ." (Mamdouh 1996, 24).

When Iqbal's husband announces to Iqbal that he has taken a second wife, we can again observe the extent to which the female suffering body exists within the body politic of patriarchy. Upon learning the news, Huda's mother retreats to her room to face her husband. She stood in front of him "worn and weary" and listened as he told her he could not stand his life with her anymore, cruelly stating that he "wanted a real woman" and "more children" (Mamdouh 1996, 37). Devastated, Iqbal kneels in front of her husband, begging him not to abandon her: "A woman may fall ill and take medicine and get well but she should never be left. Good God, Jamouli. Is this my reward?" she cries out. But Jamouli continues to blame his wife: "You've been ill for years. All that medicine and all the expense, and you're still the same" (Mamdouh 1996, 37). In closing, he demands that his wife return to her parents' house because she is no longer of any use.

Just as Huda's traumatized subjectivity divides her in two, so her critical perspective on Iqbal's distress is similarly split between perception and memory, the traumatic kernel of the real and the consolatory ideal. As her father abuses her mother, Huda observes how her mother beats her legs, scratches her thighs, curls on the ground, and shrieks. Yet, at the same time, she remembers how Iqbal used to rub her father's body, how she had whetted his appetite for sleep and snoring, covered him, and gazed at him (Mamdouh 1996, 41). By juxtaposing what we might call her mother's two bodies—the social and the physical, the ideal and the real, the submissive maternal wife and the abject, wounded animal—the novel all the more clearly exposes not simply the cruelty of Huda's father but the remorseless binary logic of patriarchy. In this society, a woman who is unable to perform the role of wife or a mother is no longer anything at all: "I am dead! I don't even have any blood left!" Iqbal exclaims as she is finally removed from the house (Mamdouh 1996, 43).

To what extent does *Mothballs* resist what we have seen to be the literary straitjacket Arabic writing imposes on the female suffering body? To be sure, the sick mother in this text is, to borrow an expression from Ann E. Kaplan, "spoken" about but rarely "speaking" (1992, 3). It is no coincidence that Iqbal is chiefly audible not through her words but her nagging, incessant cough. After she is forcibly dragged from the house, it is the silencing of this cough, more than anything else, that marks her absence: Huda relates how her mother's "coughing sounded beyond the doorway and was heard no more" (Mamdouh 1996, 43). Like the other representations of female physical illness we have examined, *Mothballs* renders the female suffering body silent and invisible. Yet, whereas Arab male writers affirm the silent presence of the sick mother—sometimes to the point of sanctifying that silence as the embodiment of female submissiveness and stoicism—*Mothballs* repeatedly undercuts this patriarchal piety. If the novel appears on the surface to reproduce the patriarchal discourse upon female physical illness—to the point where even Huda describes her mother as "a mythological figure stripped of all her roles" (Mamdouh 1996, 29)—it also interrogates that dominant mythology. The sick mother is no longer a figure to be venerated. In fact, Huda clearly resents Iqbal's subservient position and the patriarchal imaginary she has internalized.

Perhaps this is why *Mothballs* ushers in a new phase in the representation of the female suffering body in Arabic literature: it allows, however symbolically, the sick mother to "speak back" to the society that excludes her through the voice of her daughter. It is through Huda's act of ventriloquizing her mother that female physical illness finds its own voice. As we will see, Huda's own narrative not only consists of an internal dialogue between her multiple traumatized selves but between her own body and that of her mother. Both Huda and Iqbal's voices are intertwined in the former's narrative, creating what Bakhtin famously calls "a dialogue between two persons in which the statements of the second speaker are omitted," but still felt. For Bakhtin, the "second speaker is present invisibly, his words are not there," yet they have "a determining influence on all the present and visible words of the first speaker" (1984, 197). In a larger sense, Mamdouh's novel is not simply Huda's own *Bildungsroman* but a work of mourning for her mother, which seeks to enter into and relive the latter's life.

If the young Huda quite literally takes the place of her mother at times—she recounts how she "grabbed" her father "by his shiny boot" when he was on the verge of attacking his wife and used it "to crouch between his legs" (Mamdouh 1996, 27)—the identification between the two operates phenomenologically, affectively, and symbolically throughout the narrative. To begin with, Huda's memories of Iqbal always contain precise anatomies of the latter's wracked body: lightless eyes, dry skin, hollow cheeks, crooked teeth, the sound of coughs, and the sight of blood (Mamdouh 1996, 5, 39). Quite literally, the particularity of the female suffering body begins to be delineated for the first time in the history of Arabic fiction. Yet, even when she is absent, Iqbal becomes omnipresent, haunting the novel like a ghost. When Huda describes the domestic space she all too briefly shares with her mother, the spatial language she deploys recognizably contains a poignant charge: spaces, rooms, objects are invested with affective power. She describes the bedroom "at the end of the hallway," away from the rest of the household, which Huda's mother occupied (Mamdouh 1996, 39). The "iron bed" that occupied half the room and the "only window, which looked out on the courtyard," but was "usually closed" (Mamdouh 1996, 39), evokes the miserable life of the woman who spent all her days in it. Similarly, the descriptions of the warped and misshapen wardrobe in her mother's room—which "erupted in its own fit of creaky coughing"—uncannily evokes the symptoms of Iqbal's own illness.

In a more profound sense still, it becomes difficult to tell where the mother's body ends and the daughter's begins. It is not simply that Huda internalizes the social stigma that comes with being the child of a chronically ill parent but that she already *is* her mother's daughter. For Huda, my "mother's lungs are diseased, and I am consumptive" (Mamdouh 1996, 59). If her mother embraces the "heritage" of her illness—roaming around the home emitting "a scent of defeat" (Mamdouh 1996, 39)—Huda imaginatively and affectively places herself within that heritage as well. The result is, not victory, but at least a more sympathetic recuperation of Iqbal's misery. In *Mothballs,* Huda becomes her mother's voice.

Salwa Bakr: *al-'Araba al-Dhahabiya la Tas'ad ila al-Sama'*

Another writer who offers a more complex female illness narrative and a more ambiguous representation of the sick mother figure is Salwa Bakr. Her famous novel *al-'Araba al-Dhahabiya la Tas'ad ila al-Sama'* (The Golden Chariot),[7] which was published in 1991, appears to obey the dominant parameters for representing the ill woman, but at the same time it also engages in the subversive mother-daughter dialogic relation that plays itself out in *Mothballs.* If the disabled mother in this text is a passive, submissive, and gentle "Angel in the House," Bakr's narrative indirectly resists and dismantles the patriarchal cultural configurations of the society within which female characters operate. In *The Golden Chariot,* the female suffering body again begins to escape from the narrative prison in which it has been incarcerated.

Set in a women's prison outside of Cairo during Jamal Abdul Nasser's period in power, the novel is narrated by Aziza, who has been imprisoned for murdering her stepfather/lover. In a flight of fantasy, Aziza decides to create the "golden chariot" of the novel's title to take her to heaven and ponders which of her fellow prisoners to take with her to freedom. As she recounts the life stories of her fellow inmates, in a style that is consciously evocative of the *Arabian Nights,* it becomes clear that all the "criminal" characters have been punished, in one way or another, because of their gender. For Bakr, "women's crimes punishable by law" are recast as "gender issues" and "gender oppression" (Harlow 1992, 151–52). If the novel is set in a place of incarceration, for example, it is ironic that Bakr's female characters "do not speak the truth until they are able to make themselves

7. For a study of Bakr's writing see Hoda Elsadda (1996).

understood in the prison, amongst other women." The prison is transformed into "a free space in which the imprisoned souls of madwomen, misfits and criminals are liberated" (Manisty 1994, 164).

What, though, of the women who do not share that space? What, in particular, of Aziza's mother, the visually disabled mother who only ever occupied the house of Aziza's childhood and womanhood, who dies early in the text and who remains a silent figure in Aziza's narrative? Why is she denied the narrative freedom afforded to the other female characters? To start with, Aziza's mother is depicted as an angelic figure whose blindness is more than compensated for by her beauty and docile temperament. It is striking, too, that her visual impairment does not (as in so many other cases we have witnessed) impair her marriage prospects. In another variation from the norm, Aziza's mother's disability is not the symbolic punishment for some moral defect: it is merely something "fate had ordained for her" because she "has been blind since birth" (Bakr 1995, 11).

To Aziza, her mother was "gentle" and her visual handicap "gave her a certain poetic aura," which made her look like "the queen of the ancient mythic world" (Bakr 1995, 11). Yet, physical blindness also leads to social blindness and, in particular, the mother's "ignorance and unawareness" of the illicit affair taking place between Aziza and her stepfather (Bakr 1995, 11). For Aziza's mother, the growing relationship between her husband and her daughter is an entirely innocent one based on fatherly affection. If Aziza's mother quite literally cannot see the transgression taking place under her own roof, her sightless eyes do not offer any kind of moral reproach to Aziza: her visual handicap defuses Aziza's guilt. In this respect, as Elizabeth G. Gitter postulates in the context of a larger discussion of literary representations of blindness, both mother and daughter effectively become invisible to one another: the daughter's actions "cannot be said to exist if [they are] not seen and acknowledged" by the world, and the mother becomes a "pure object incapable of subjectivity" (1999, 685).

Although Aziza's descriptions of her mother's visual handicap are devoid of the stigmatizations that generally attach themselves to physically sick and disabled female characters, her illness narrative is (understandably) still permeated with an irreducible sense of shame. For Gitter, sightlessness may well shelter the guilty party from the "punishing . . .

gaze," but it also "arouses a profound uneasiness and poses a powerful symbolic threat." The "passive blinded eye is the symbol of punishment enacted," Gitter argues, and equally, we might add, of Aziza's own future punishment. Perhaps more disturbingly, Aziza's mother's blindness signifies both her own isolation and her daughter's impending removal from society: "The bland enucleated eye of the blind represents both an annihilation of the self and a terrifying exile from human community" (Gitter 1999, 684–85). In the remainder of this novel, Aziza will attempt to restore both herself and her mother from this state of total de-subjectification.

For Bakr, then, the disabled mother figure is every bit as ambiguous and problematic a trope as it is in Mamdouh. On the one hand, her text perpetuates the traditional patriarchal representation of female illness and disability. But, on the other, it deconstructs this image of sentimental domesticity by depicting this trope as a potential threat to the social stability of the domestic space that mother, daughter, and stepfather occupy. To start with, the mother's literal blindness reflects her symbolic blindness toward what is taking place under her own roof. By the same token, this same blindness underscores her failure to exert even a minimal level of influence over the household. If Aziza takes responsibility for her relationship with her stepfather, there is also a sense in which she blames her mother for the latter's failure to stop her: the mother "never tried to listen or use her other senses to detect what her eyes failed to distinguish" (Bakr 1995, 186). By so completely living up to the patriarchal image of the submissive, angelic mother figure, Aziza's mother ironically fails to meet her *real* responsibilities toward her daughter. The sick mother in *The Golden Chariot* is a failure—not because she is unable to perform her traditional role—but because she performs it too well.

If Bakr's novel demythologizes the traditional patriarchal discourse in which the female suffering body is enmeshed, it also seeks new ways to represent that body. It continually seeks to rescue the mother's body from its physical and social marginalization and locates it firmly in the center of the narrative. As Hafez argues in a different context, the novel resorts to "a significant technique which acknowledges the absence of the woman and turns it with the dexterity of narrative treatment into a sign of her overwhelming presence" (1995, 172). Like Mamdouh, Bakr recuperates the absent mother figure by means of Aziza's own intensely dialogic narrative voice: the mother's presence is felt through the imaginary conversations that Aziza conducts with her in the prison ward. In creating a narrative about her fellow inmates, she also creates a maternal voice to address and engage in dialogue with because her mother had no real voice in her life and because the daughter pines for her mother's physical and emotional presence: we are told that nothing was ever heard from Aziza's prison ward except the "extended conversations with her mother," and her murdered husband (Bakr 1995, 183).

Perhaps most powerfully of all, Aziza's betrayal of her mother—via her illicit relationship with her stepfather—even becomes a point of imagined solidarity between the two. To give a voice to her mother, Aziza has to situate her mother's biography in what Jo Malin would call a "textual relationship next to [and] overlapping" with her own story (2000, 6). When Aziza recounts her growing relationship with her stepfather, she also enters into imaginative empathy with her mother: she had "joined her mother in bestowing her abundant affection upon the beloved man." She goes on to add that "both of them had inhabited the narrow world of two women restricted by the four walls of the large, old house . . ." and remembers how the two women prepared themselves for their beloved's arrival. Aziza would adorn flattering nightgowns and set free her locks "just like her mother" (Bakr 1995, 12). For Bakr's protagonist, mother and daughter become "partners of the same body and companions of days past" (Bakr 1995, 186).

This "triangular Oedipus situation," to borrow a phrase from Nancy Chodorow's study of mothering (1978, 140), is not simply a source of familial strife but of imagined unity. According to Chodorow, the daughter's turn to the father is as much a question of the former's relation to her mother as her father (1978, 149): what is at stake is not simply the development of a new sexual orientation but the "creation of a feminine sense of self-in-relationship" (1978, 137). For Bakr, Aziza's relationship with her father/stepfather is both an act of aggression toward her mother and perversely an act of love for her. The protagonist oscillates between feelings of anger with regard to her mother's physical and social absence and a desire to "identify with her mother in their common feminine inferiority

. . ." (Chodorow 1978, 138–39). In this highly ambivalent sense, the Oedipal moment is both Aziza's assertion of independence from the mother and an attempt to put herself in the place where the latter's absent body should be.

In *The Golden Chariot*, then, Bakr simultaneously demythologizes the female suffering body and seeks to imaginatively repossess it in order to restore its lost physical and symbolic agency. By becoming the mistress of her stepfather, Aziza allows her body to become a surrogate for her mother's own body both when alive and dead. Yet, by murdering her stepfather when he takes a second wife, Aziza both castrates the embodiment of patriarchy and destroys the patriarchal ideal of womanhood to which her mother succumbed. For Aziza, murdering her stepfather becomes the ultimate act of allegiance to her mother: it is both a surrogate act of revenge for his original betrayal of her mother and a symbolic act of atonement for her own complicity. If previous illness narratives have sought to marginalize the sick mother figure, then, *The Golden Chariot* admits her to the center of the narrative. It is what Malin would call "a hybrid form of autobiographical narrative containing an embedded narrative of the mother" (2000, 11). In Aziza's story of her childhood, her love affair, and murder, the sick mother also begins to speak.

Speaking Daughters/Subjective Bodies

In the narratives analyzed thus far in this chapter, the mother-daughter relationship begins to shape new realities in the representation of physically ill/disabled women and in their ensuing illness narratives. For Mamdouh and Bakr, in particular, the struggle to give voice and meaning to the sick mother's experience forges new narrative structures that see the daughter not only observing the ill/disabled body from the outside but seeking to embody it herself imaginatively and affectively. If later narratives continue to explore the mother-daughter dynamic, they also add a new dimension to the relationship: Egyptian Miral al-Tahawy's first novel *al-Khiba'*, for example, explicitly interrogates the very discourses of health, illness, and disability we have sought to address in this book. In *al-Khiba'*, we also encounter another first in the Arabic novel: the attempt to render the subjective experience of what it means and feels like to be a woman who suffers from a physical illness/disability.

Miral al-Tahawy: *al-Khiba'*

To be sure, *al-Khiba'* (The Tent, 1996) focuses on the life and world of the Bedouin and, particularly, of Bedouin women. Its main character is Fatima, a young girl who—like the narrator of *Mothballs*—reacts against her family, upbringing, and environment. As well as Fatima, the family consists of an ailing mother, three sisters, and an over-powering grandmother who (in the absence of the father) rules over them all with an iron grip. Both unable to live within her oppressive environment and incapable of breaking free of it altogether, Fatima gradually descends into solitude, illusion, and madness. In addition to its harrowing portrait of mental illness, however, al-Tahawy's novel chronicles Fatima's growing physical disability after an accident and the impact it has upon her, her family, and her culture more widely.

Early in the novel, Fatima injures her leg when, despite her grandmother's warnings, she climbs a tree and falls. To begin with, the leg is merely massaged and wrapped in rags, and the young girl continues to go about her daily activities. However, the injury does not heal and, later, the leg has to be amputated. While the narrative principally focuses on Fatima's mental degeneration, her physical incapacity also plays a significant role in the text: both feed into a larger meditation upon the relationship between the ill/disabled body and the social body or the body politic. In Fatima's case, her physical disability not only heightens her existing sense of social oppression but becomes the object of a new set of reflections on what it means to be "disabled."

However, it is also clear from her defiance of her grandmother's orders when climbing the tree that the young girl refuses to abide by patriarchal norms that dictate how boys and girls should play and behave. Fatima's lost leg is a marker of, and a challenge to, the predominant discourse of womanhood. Even when still a child, she realizes that she is burdened by bodily restrictions because of who she is and what she represents. For Fatima, such gender anxieties are heightened through her relationship with her sick mother. By becoming disabled herself, Fatima symbolically repeats the fate of her mother and extends the lineage of the female suffering body. In this respect, *The Tent* already constitutes a significant departure from, and extension of, the dominant representation of female physical disability: the illness narrative is no longer localized in the body of the mother but extends to encompass the corporeal space of the daughter as well.

At the beginning of the narrative, Fatima is already aware that something is not "right" about her mother. It appears that the woman's inability to produce male offspring has brought social shame upon her and sickened her body and self. Like *Layla Wahida*, al-Tahawy's novel links women's health to her reproductive capacities but with a significant twist: *The Tent* posits that it is the *sex* of the child that determines the physical fitness of the mother. To this extent, Fatima's mother is someone who has only "brought grief" to those around her (al-Tahawy 1998, 66). She is, as her mother-in-law proclaims, "a deranged woman" who has "given birth to nothing but bad luck" (al-Tahawy 1998, 9). For Fatima herself, her mother is a timid, fragile, and sick creature whose presence generates nothing but foreboding in her youngest daughter: the early mornings were full of "anxiety and tension," because her "mother wouldn't open the door of her room, or, if she did open it" she gazed at her children with "apprehensive eyes." The mother was a "pale, emaciated figure, the thin veins on the eyelids swollen from floods of tears," an image which "choked [Fatima's] heart with sadness" (al-Tahawy 1998, 9). In response to her mother's "helpless eyes," Fatima was filled with pity but still she fled "from the stench of tears" (al-Tahawy 1998, 4).

Due to her intimate exposure to illness and disability at such an early age, Fatima's understanding of female sexuality is inextricably connected to a sense of despair, anguish, and even violence. When she overhears the sounds of her parents' lovemaking, she confuses it with cries of pain. Fatima tells of her father entering her mother's room and of "the muffled sound which turned into a terrible inconsolable sobbing" afterward. She even begins to believe one of the female slave's claims that her father is "strangling" her mother. Just as when she ignored her grandmother's orders and climbed the tree, the young girl feels the intense urge to run away (al-Tahawy 1998, 38). The persistent desire to keep moving and, in particular, to leave behind the borders of the house, stem from her desire to break free of a future she sees awaiting her in the form of her mother's body. In the end, however, Fatima cannot escape her mother's fate and the two women's lives are interlinked by a shared sense of social alienation and oppression.

Like her mother before her, Fatima is blamed by the family for causing her own disability. When she takes refuge in a well, her grandmother proclaims the girl is trouble because she is "crippled and possessed" (al-Tahawy 1998, 41). The reality, however, is that Fatima's condition is caused by her desperate attempt to flee the suffering of her mother and the suffering that awaits her as a woman. After all, allusions to her mother's sobbing and how much it pained her are more than once paralleled with descriptions of her own attempts to find refuge in the well: Fatima describes that she crawled despite the "thorns against [her] legs and the blood perhaps drying on the bandages" (al-Tahawy, 39). But her mother's sobbing follows her wherever she goes.

For al-Tahawy, Fatima's dilemma is how she can bond with her mother's sick body while simultaneously removing herself from its fate. Fatima repeatedly attempts to exclude her mother's story from the narrative in favor of tales of her grandmother and the other women around her. It is clearly easier for her to speak of the grandmother's over-bearing presence than the mother's distant, victimized, and sickly state. Yet, by injuring her leg, becoming disabled, and gradually slipping into insanity, the daughter's life course inevitably means that the repressed figure of the mother returns. In other words, Fatima acts out the script of her mother's absent narrative through her own body: the mother's fragile, vulnerable, and helpless body is reproduced in Fatima's own limping, crawling, hopping body that had no one to "carry" it (al-Tahawy 1998, 108).

The narrative in *The Tent* thus turns full circle as Fatima's desperate attempts to escape ultimately leave her in the same position as her mother. At the end of the text, the protagonist realizes that she had become the same pathetic figure who used to haunt her own childhood: "I had entered the chamber of sobbing silence. The same swollen eyes" (al-Tahawy 1998, 124). Elsewhere, she acknowledges that children were now making "fun of my deformity. They say I'm possessed" (al-Tahawy 1998, 130). The young protagonist's fate is a poignant testament to how physical disability impedes the aspiration to personal freedom, autonomy, and self-determination, but it is also an indictment of the oppression imposed by traditional discourses of what female bodies should be and how they should perform. In this sense, Fatima's tragedy is not simply an inability to overcome the physical immobility imposed by her own disability but an inability to escape the psychological and social immobility imposed by her family history.

If *The Tent* is ultimately a somber narrative about the impossibility of ever escaping a traumatic past, Fatima's narration of her own life and re-narration of her mother's once again permits the female suffering body to speak. By making her own body the stage for the drama of her mother's life, Fatima's narrative quite literally *re-embodies* the maternal suffering body and rescues it from the alterity to which it had been consigned. Perhaps, in this sense, Fatima's madness is not merely an indictment of her oppressive community but the continuation of her lonely struggle for independence. When she opts to live outside the family house in a small tent with only her maid and an imagined ghost for company, Fatima continues to defy norms just as she had done when she first climbed the tree: she becomes "her own darling and no one else's darling, darling of her own anger, and her own sad nights . . ." (al-Tahawy 1998, 126).

What does *The Tent*'s illness narrative add to the mother-daughter dynamic so subtly explored in *Mothballs* and *The Golden Chariot*? To be sure, Fatima's narrative dialogically recuperates the absent mother in the same way as the early texts. Yet, we can also identify a significant number of departures in the representation of the female suffering body. Firstly, al-Tahawy's mother-daughter dialogue transpires between *two* suffering bodies and, consequently, the exchange between them is not merely symbolic or imagined but affective and embodied. By seeking to re-narrate the story of her mother, Fatima is not simply seeking to imagine another woman's suffering, but to make sense of her own, equally real, pain. Such a genuinely double-voiced corporeal collage produces a remarkably rich narrative that is capable of exploring every aspect of illness whether affective, phenomenological, social, or ideological. Finally, it is important to note that the novel is one of the few texts of the 1990s to offer a self-conscious exploration of what it means to be physically disabled both from a corporeal and a social perspective. In this respect, *The Tent* succeeds where its tragic protagonist fails and breaks free of the patriarchal stranglehold upon representations of female physical illness and disability: it transforms the female suffering body from what Mary Poovey calls the object "of another's discourse," into "women as subjects of their own," capable of speaking about their bodies in the first person (1990, 29).

Domestic Representations/Oppositional Dynamics

In our analysis of the representation of female physical illness/disability in male writing between 1950 and 2000, we saw that a number of tropes predominate: the "fallen" woman, the embodiment of the nation in crisis, and the ideal mother/wife. It is now possible to add a further trope to our taxonomy following our analysis of Arab women's writing in the same period: the sick mother. As this chapter has shown, the protagonist of *Layla Wahida* understands her infertility as sickness, the sick women in *Habbat al-Naftaleen* (Mothballs) and *al-'Araba* (The Golden Chariot) are both mother figures, while *al-Khiba'* (The Tent) concerns the relationship between a sick mother and her disabled daughter. For women authors in this period, it is also striking that one particular form of illness/disability is singled out for attention: blindness. In *Fi al-Layl*, we saw that the young protagonist is blind while the sick mother in *The Golden Chariot* suffers from the same condition.

It is clear from this brief overview that representations of the female suffering body by women writers still remain largely confined to the domestic sphere. The ill woman does not, in the end, escape the home in which male writers had so forcefully placed her. As we have seen, all the texts in this chapter situate the female body—ill or healthy—against the backdrop of a larger set of debates about the role and nature of womanhood in Arab society. If many of the female characters in these novels are forced to conform to a certain idea of womanhood, the ill/disabled woman is damned because of her inability to meet the stringent test for femininity set by patriarchy. In this respect, it is little wonder that the tone of many of the works discussed in this chapter shuttles between pathos and anger, between resignation and resistance, between a feeling of worthlessness and a rage against the men who decide who or what is worthy in the first place.

However, despite or because of their limitations, female illness narratives are ultimately more complex and variegated than those of their male counterparts. On the one hand, they appear to conform to the dominant patriarchal ideology that excludes the female body in pain. On the other, though, they also succeed in constructing embedded narratives that resist such acts of textual erasure. In this chapter, we have seen that female illness narratives are characterized by opposing forces, discourse, or narrative trajectories which seek to *both* internalize patriarchal representations of female physical illness *and* offer a radical counter-history which gives voice to silent suffering.

To be sure, earlier narratives like *Fi al-Layl* and *Layla Wahida* do not appear to depart radically with the prevailing rhetoric and ideology of illness/disability. Written in the 1950s and 1960s, respectively, at a time when women's writing was just beginning to find a place in the Arab literary world, the two novels' representations of the physically ill and disabled figure undoubtedly break the silence surrounding sick female bodies. They also reveal the extent to which any comprehension of female physical illness could only take place within a larger patriarchal discourse of women's fertility, reproduction, and so on. Ultimately, however, the works fail to address the question of the sick female body in depth: Nuwaylati and Khoury's representation of sick women remain too close to the patriarchal ideology they seek to resist. In classic Bakhtinian terms, they remain monologic narratives that are unable to let the ill female speak in her own voice.

The appearance of texts like al-Shaykh's *Faras al-Shaytan* in the 1970s, however, saw this conspiracy of silence surrounding ill female bodies gradually breaking down. Although the novel only sketches the illness and death of the mother figure, it still exposes and denounces the cruelty and hypocrisy of patriarchal authority. However, despite its powerful exploration of how the mother's absence impacts her daughter, the novel stops short of venturing into the world of the sick mother herself. In a similar vein to Nuwaylati and Khoury, al-Shaykh's illness narrative leaves the sick mother's bodily experience of pain unvoiced either by herself or her daughter.

When a new set of female illness narratives emerged in the 1980s and 1990s, though, the female suffering body finally began to articulate itself. In works such as *Mothballs, The Golden Chariot,* and *The Tent,* a genuinely dialogic mother-daughter narrative starts to appear that renders the sick mother a textual, affective, and social presence in her daughter's life. By rewriting the patriarchal trope of the sick mother, by calling attention to her textual silence, and allowing that silence to resonate, and by finally allowing that figure to speak, Mamdouh, Bakr, and al-Tahawy's narratives challenge the marginalization of female physical illness/disability and establish a new dialogue with the female suffering body.

What form does this dialogue take? It is true enough that there is nothing inherently dialogic—in Bakhtin's sense of the term—about representations of the mother-daughter relationship. For Marianne Hirsch, such representations in feminist narratives suffer from a tendency to always assume the perspective of the growing child at the expense of the mother: the mother's part in that process "remains absent, erased from theatrical and narrative representation" (1989, 169). The majority of the female texts discussed in this chapter chart out a similar mother-daughter narrative where the sick woman/mother is not a speaking subject and her experience with illness is mediated purely through a daughter's point of view. Perhaps more importantly, there is also a power dynamic to the relationship: the daughter struggles to embody the mother's agency without annihilating her own autonomy. In spite of such caveats, though, the mother-daughter narratives discussed here overcome such dualisms: the sick mother finds a voice through a daughter who is aware of her mother's suffering and is forced to identify with it.[8]

8. Perhaps it is worth recalling Hélène Cixous's classic account of the affirmative relationship between the maternal body and feminine writing. For Cixous, women acquire a voice from the mother: "A woman is never far from 'mother.' . . . There is always within her at least a little of that good mother's milk. She writes in white ink" (1976, 881). In the same vein, she argues that "the Dark Continent" of the female body/mother's body is *"neither dark nor unexplorable"*: "it is still unexplored only because we have been made to believe that it is too dark to be explorable" (1976, 884–85). This argument could be extended to incorporate

For Mamdouh, Bakr, and al-Tahawy, we might say that the sick mother becomes a species of "intersubject" situated within and between her own subjectivity and that of her daughter. Reading their novels, we encounter not a single voice but a double one that, in turn, speaks to the dialogism of the world around it: Bakhtin famously argues that "the living utterance" cannot but "brush up against thousands of living dialogic threads, woven by socio-ideological consciousness" that makes it "an active participant in social dialogue" (1981, 276–77). By exposing the dialogism at the heart of society itself, the novels also speak back to the monologism of patriarchy that silenced women in the first place. In a word, the mother-daughter dialogue becomes a model for that larger polyphony of voices, lives, worlds, and bodies that Bakhtin famously calls "social heteroglossia" (1981, 324).[9]

If mother-daughter narratives often depict the daughter's struggle for autonomy, what is striking in these texts is the extent to which the mother becomes vital to her child's achievement of agency. Far from impeding the daughter's own subjectivity, the relation to the mother becomes a necessary precondition to it. By repeatedly situating the marginal ill female figure at the center of their fiction, these writers—according to Hite's analysis of women's writing—"decenter an inherited narrative structure and undermine the values informing this structure" (1989, 24). For Bakhtin, writing about maternal biographies in his essay "Author and Hero in Aesthetic Activity," this displacement of existing narrative structures even extends to the figure of the female narrator herself. Bakhtin argues that there is an ambiguity surrounding the precise identity of the protagonist

---

the even "darker" continent that is the female suffering body in Arabic literature: it begins to find a voice and language through the narratives of speaking daughters.

9. In his classic analysis, Bakhtin identifies heteroglossia as *"another's speech in another's language,* serving to express authorial intentions but in a refracted way." He adds that "such speech constitutes a special type of *double-voiced discourse"* since it "serves two speakers at the same time and expresses simultaneously two different intentions." Furthermore, Bakhtin asserts that, in this discourse, "there are two voices, two meanings and two expressions" and these are "dialogically interrelated" (1981, 324).

in biographies of mothers written by daughters. When women write about their mother's life, the latter's story permeates the daughter's narrative: the mother is the voice that resides in all of us (Bakhtin 1990, 152–53). In his account, such texts possess what Bakhtin calls a "relational rather than alienational otherness" which undermines the "monologic" strategy of "accomplishment and great deed" that is more often found in male writings (Malin 2000, 10).

Perhaps this "relational alterity" described by Bakhtin also captures the complex interaction of same and other that takes place in the maternal illness narratives that comprise *Mothballs*, *The Golden Chariot*, and *The Tent*. It is clear that all three novels address the question of how to "create a perspective" for the silent mother figure and "create the situation and necessary conditions for it to sound" (Bakhtin, 1981, 358). As we have seen, each text stages what Bakhtin calls "an encounter" or a "hybridization" of two languages "co-existing within the boundaries of a single dialect" of gender identity (Bakhtin 1981, 358–59). For Mamdouh, Bakr, and al-Tahawy, this encounter takes place in uncanny spaces, voices, and modes: architectural spaces (*Mothballs*), imagined conversations (*The Golden Chariot*) and the intimate corporeality of ill bodies (*Mothballs* and *The Tent*).

While the physically ill/disabled female figure remains silent, each novel posits this silence not simply as an absence but as a mode of repressed, inarticulate speech. Reading Virginia Woolf's novels, Patricia Ondek Laurence argues that Woolf transmits the "unsaid, unspoken and unsayable" in her work (1991, 3), by constructing "a narrative space for silence" that allows it to be heard *as* silence (1991, 7). By the same logic, Mamdouh, Bakr, and al-Tahawy's representations of the sick mother "reposition this silent, seemingly passive, absent woman in literature and life" as an individual whose world has not—so far—been "disclosed" (1991, 57). Such representations demythologize what Luce Irigaray has called "the masculine imagery" in which female physical illness and disability have been enshrouded and expose the "way it has reduced women to silence" (Irigaray 1985, 164). In narrating the life of the sick woman through the focalization of her daughter, the sick woman is—if not quite given back her voice—at least permitted the eloquence of her silence.

Finally, however, this chapter has also borne witness to the emergence of the *speaking* female body in pain. In al-Tahawy's *The Tent,* female physical illness and disability begins to be articulated via the mother and daughter's *shared* experience of sickness. It is this sense of solidarity that finally collapses the subject/object dualism of mother-daughter illness narratives and permits a genuine intersubjective female suffering body to be produced. For al-Tahawy's narrator, the female suffering body finally begins to speak, not simply through the voice of a husband, father, or even a daughter, but in her own voice. By allowing the daughter to articulate not just her mother's but her *own* experience of illness and disability, the female body in pain is finally written into existence.

In conclusion, then, this chapter has shown that Arab women's writing between 1950 and 2000 simultaneously perpetuates *and* breaks with the dominant norms for representing female physical illness and disability we delineated in the last chapter. To be sure, Arab women writers—like their male counterparts—are often less interested in the female suffering body in itself than as a social or political cipher. It is also true that—again like their male equivalents—they police the narrative space around that body very carefully and do not permit it the textual freedom to embody itself. Yet, at the same time, Arab women's writing does, finally, write the body in pain into recognition. By attending to what Elaine Showalter calls "the holes in discourse, the blanks and gaps and silences" in the "prison house" of language that surrounds female physical illness and disability (1985, 255), Arab women's fiction offers a new portal into the representation of the suffering woman. For the women writers represented in this chapter, then, the ill/disabled woman's body is simultaneously marginalized *and* dramatically transformed, or, better, transformed *through* the very recognition and production of her thoroughgoing marginalization. If we may briefly return to Foucault's genealogy of power/knowledge, what the works discussed in this chapter exemplify is the famous axiom from *The History of Sexuality*: "Where there is power, there is resistance, and yet, or rather consequently, this resistance is never in a position of exteriority in relation to power" (1990, 95). Just as it is in the history of sexuality, so it is in the history of female illness and disability: resistance to the patriarchal power over female physical illness and disability begins from *within* that power. The true achievements of the writers discussed in this chapter are both to lay bare that power and, for the first time, to reveal the fragile economy of body, affect, and pain that it seeks to oppress. In this way, Arab women's writing from 1950 to 2000 creates the space in which, as we will see in the next chapter, the female suffering body can begin to speak for itself.

RE-WRITING THE SUFFERING BODY

2000–

In contemporary Arabic literature, the female suffering body finally completes its journey from a silent, indeed absent, subject to a fully articulated and embodied agent. It ceases to be merely a signifier for some apparently more urgent socio-political trauma and becomes a physical, affective, and phenomenological state of being in its own right. For the writers under discussion in this chapter—both female and, to a lesser extent, male—I wish to argue that female physical illness and disability is no longer subordinated to some social, sexual, or maternal ideal—but tackled head-on and permitted to speak in its own voice. If we can adopt a Foucauldian vocabulary, we might argue that contemporary Arabic literature witnesses the birth of a new object of power/knowledge: the female suffering body. This chapter will offer a genealogy of the emergence of that body in Lebanese Hassan Daoud's *Makyaj Khafif li-Hadhih al-Layla*, Iraqi Betool Khedairi's *Ghayib*, and Syrian Haifa' Bitar's *Imra'a Min Hadha al-'Asr.*

Aesthetic Visibility

Hassan Daoud: *Makyaj Khafif li-Hadhih al-Layla*

In his considerable body of work, the eminent Lebanese novelist Hassan Daoud focuses upon the lives of individuals on the margins of society: the Shi'ite Muslim immigrants in *Binayat Matild* (The House of Mathilde, 1983), the aged man in *Ayyam Za'ida* (Borrowed Time, 1990), and the physically disabled male protagonist in *Ghina' al-Batriq* (The Penguin's Song, 1998). According to Samira Aghacy, his writing is also remarkable for what it does not depict: Daoud, unlike contemporaries such as Rachid al-Daif and Elias Khoury, does not deal directly with the Lebanese Civil War (2000, 205).[1] However, in spite of the fact that the war is largely absent from Daoud's work, Elise Salem argues that this absence is often "revelatory" because it "certainly feels like [Daoud's work] is set in the miserable war-torn" period (2003, 169), adding that "one need not resort to a landscape of actual war to depict destruction, death and tragedy" (2003, 172). For Ken Seigneurie, as well, Daoud remains implicitly, if not explicitly, a war novelist through his exploitation of the "ruins" motif: Daoud's *The House of Mathilde* (1999) uses the trope of the ruined building as an "allegory of the destruction of the nation" (2008, 54).[2]

It is important to note that this early use of the trope of ruins is extended to the male body in later novels: both the old man in *Borrowed Time* (2009) and the physically impaired male character in *Ghina' al-Batriq* are brutalized, either by their family and/or by society at large. Accordingly, their physical state parallels the state of the nation. Yet, in the recent novel *Makyaj Khafif li-Hadhih al-Layla* (Light Makeup for Tonight, 2003), Daoud extends the trope of physical ruin to the female body. In this text, Daoud focuses on the subjectivity of one disabled Lebanese woman and, by immersing himself imaginatively in the protagonist's relation to her scarred body, turns *Makyaj Khafif* into a new kind of illness narrative.

As we will see, *Makyaj Khafif* marks a significant shift in the passage to subjectivity of ill/disabled female bodies in contemporary Arabic literature. In Fadia Nassar, the central character around whom the whole narrative is built, Daoud provides an account of the female disabled body which, as Lynda Nead puts it in a different context, exposes that body's "social and psychic formation": the novel accommodates "both the

1. For a study of crisis and memory in the work of al-Daif see Paul Starkey (2003).

2. For a study of the ruin motif in Lebanese literature, film, and culture see Ken Seigneurie (2011).

inscription of its external surface and the production of its internal psychic operations" (2007, 71). To quickly rehearse the plot, Fadia is caught up in a bomb explosion and, as a result, falls into a two-month coma. When she wakes up, she discovers that she has lost her husband, a sister, and a brother. She also finds herself to be disabled, with severe scarring from her neck all the way down her lower body, a limp, and a hoarse voice that seems to whistle every time she speaks. Finally, Fadia has also lost all memory of the three years of her life before the bomb.

After her trauma, Jihan—a childhood friend and a filmmaker—finds the raw material for a story in Fadia's life and proposes to make a documentary film about her. Thus, the novel unfolds with Fadia describing her life, or what she remembers of it, to Jihan. Yet, on another level, the novel also explores the burgeoning relationship between Fadia and a painter Youssef, who executes a number of nude paintings of her. In short, Fadia's process of coming to terms with her new identity (or lack of it) as a disabled woman is staged between two distinct aesthetic processes—painting and cinema—which allow her to become both a spectacle and the spectator of her own body.

During the novel, Daoud offers a powerful depiction of the phenomenology of physical disability. For Fadia, her disability has rendered her an incomplete and almost illusory entity—as if she exists only as a vestige of the woman she once was. She divides her identity into the selves who existed before and after the explosion: the protagonist speaks of living a "second life" after the trauma. The person she was before the explosion remains out of reach "on the other side of the border" (Daoud 2003, 22–23). In addition to this sense of bereavement for the person she once was, however, Fadia is also, of course, in mourning for her husband. She is the last remaining "trace of [the] dead man" (Daoud 2003, 20).

To counteract this sense of physical and psychological lack, Fadia struggles to literally and symbolically put her body back together. She painstakingly attempts to re-synchronize her movements: her walk, the way in which she offers her hand for greeting, and the manner in which she sits down on the sofa are carefully carried out in slow motion to regain the impression of being "whole" (Daoud 2003, 19–20). However, the low voice which barely comes out in a whisper, the scar which Fadia knows extends all the way to her lower body—and which she compares to a "dress zipper" that hides beneath it things that have been "torn and cut"—betray the pretence of normality she wishes to establish (Daoud 2003, 12). Both her voice and scar also heighten the spectral quality of her appearance.

Even the pleasure she experiences in her physical relationship with Youssef has a vague, half-finished feel. When describing their sexual encounters, Fadia says Youssef and she existed as "strangers when they were doing it and remain[ed] strangers afterward." For Fadia, sex merely compounds the sense of lack or emptiness she feels: "I reached . . . the point we were supposed to reach, but what I felt with him was little," she recollects, almost as if her body could not "catch up with her desire." In the end, what she is left with is merely the trace of a pleasure that requires more time to become "complete" (Daoud 2003, 43).

Yet, in addition to her attempts to physically reconstruct her old body, the novel also depicts Fadia's efforts to symbolically testify to the birth of her new one. It is telling that she insists that Jihan's documentary film should begin with the day she was released from the hospital (Daoud 2003, 25). By wanting to star in a film that will capture the story of her life, Fadia betrays a wish to see herself and be seen by others in her new body, with all its scars and physical impairments. As Fadia narrates, edits, then reconstructs the story of her life to Jihan, she observes herself captured on screen and shifts from being the spectacle to the spectator.[3] When she watches a rehearsal shot of herself driving a car, for example, she confesses that she had been in dire need of seeing her new self in order to come to terms with how others would see her (Daoud 2003, 36). The very presence of Jihan's camera bestows a certain dignity and importance: Fadia admits that she likes the fact that "someone was busy with her" and that "someone would see in her something worth filming and watching" (Daoud 2003, 77). In a more symbolic sense, the protagonist's desire to star in her own film is also part and parcel of Daoud's attempt to defy what we

3. For a discussion of the politics of female spectatorship in films see Mary Ann Doane (1981).

have seen to be the prevailing aesthetic representation of women in Arab culture and, particularly, of ill or disabled women.[4]

When filming Fadia, Jihan colludes in her attempt to deconstruct the dominant cultural ideal of female beauty. By consistently emphasizing the former's disability—the awkward walk brought about by the accident and the reverberations of a voice that whispered and whistled when speaking (Daoud 2003, 129–30)—the filmmaker seeks to reveal the intimacy of Fadia's suffering body. Even more, Jihan's camera juxtaposes Fadia's current, disabled body with her previous, culturally "ideal" one. To borrow John Rajchman's term, Jihan shoots "before-and-after pictures" that reveal how Fadia moved from one physical reality to another (1988, 90). For Jihan, the aesthetic decision to chronicle Fadia's life before the accident also provides the latter with a narrative structure through which to understand her trauma. In depicting the passage from Fadia's childhood, through her role as a wife and a mother, all the way up to her current physical alienation from the world around her, Jihan's film almost becomes an alternative narrative through which we can seek the "authentic" Fadia.

For a novelist like Daoud, however, it goes without saying that the struggle to put Fadia back together again—whether physically or aesthetically—inevitably remains fraught with ambiguity. To what extent is such a literal or symbolic act of reconstruction possible? Is Fadia merely consoling herself with the attention of Jihan's camera lens? Or is Jihan's film merely exploiting Fadia for the former's own aesthetic purposes? To be sure, Jihan undoubtedly seeks to bear witness to the "real" Fadia, but the film itself testifies to the impossibility of such an endeavor. It is arguable that, by allowing both Fadia's daughter and a professional actress to play Fadia at different stages of her life, Jihan produces yet another aesthetic exclusion of the female suffering body. After all, Fadia's body is displaced onto two other bodies who become, to borrow Kaja Silverman's term, "representation[s] of a representation" (1988, 3). Even Fadia herself comes to feel alienated from her "own" film when Jihan makes the decision to limit her appearances on screen to very short, fragmentary

4. See Nead (2007, 60–70).

scenes. Perhaps, though, it is this very failure of representation that ultimately makes the film all the more intimate, if painful, an experience for the protagonist: Jihan permits Fadia to enter into a "visual confrontation with [her] own lack" (Silverman 1988, 19). When observing her daughter playing herself at a younger age, Fadia becomes intensely conscious of her current physical "inferiority" in contrast to her symbolic younger self: she confesses that she has become acutely aware of what she had lost (Daoud 2003, 73). In the end, Fadia gives up hope that the film can restore her body to herself: she recoils from the scrutiny of the camera lens and rejects the film as a misrepresentation of her life and her body.

Why, ultimately, is Jihan seeking to film Fadia's suffering body? It gradually becomes clear that her decision to occlude Fadia's presence is merely the prelude to a much more powerful and intimate aesthetic "reveal": Fadia's body will be returned to its rightful owner in a series of scenes that will depict her as she really is now, without any makeup or disguise. For Jihan, Fadia will be allowed to tell her own story—including the story of the night of the bomb—as the camera's eye wanders over her body and over the defining spaces of her life. By showing the place where the bomb exploded, Jihan wants to make visible what Rajchman would call Fadia's "being in space": "[I]t is not simply a matter of what a building shows 'symbolically' or 'semiotically' but also what it makes visible about us and within us" (1988, 103). In this respect, it could be argued that Jihan's film turns inside out the classic representation of the disabled body as cipher for a wounded body politic. It is no longer a question of what Fadia's body tells us about her environment, but about what her environment tells us about her own intimate physical and psychological state.

If Jihan sees her film as an attempt to challenge hegemonic representations of female illness and disability—and to allow the female suffering body to speak for itself—Fadia, by contrast, perceives it as yet another oppressive attempt to fictionalize that body and, consequently, she resists the filmmaker's gaze. It is to her painter/lover Youssef, and his own attempt to "frame" the female body, that Fadia next chooses to reveal herself. As Jihan films Fadia's story, Youssef paints her body: he, tellingly, is interested in her as a purely corporeal being. For Fadia, the experience of posing naked and baring all her scars to the gaze of the male artist, and of watching as that body is transformed on canvas into the object of the gaze, brings about a remarkable transformation in her self-image. Just like Jihan's film, Youssef's attempt to capture Fadia on canvas overturns the patriarchal discourse surrounding the ill/disabled female body. What was once rendered invisible now becomes visible for the first time.

By stripping the body of all the signifiers of femininity—heavy makeup, layers of clothing, and so on—Youssef's painting reveals the materiality of that body with all the signs of violence that mar its surface. When looking over the first painting that Youssef completes, Fadia sees the "long, strong" scar that extends from her neck to her lower body: Youssef has deliberately accentuated it to the point that it seems as if it were protruding out of the painting (Daoud 2003, 81). Fadia also notes that the woman in the painting is depicted as staring defiantly back at the observer as if she refuses to be reduced to the passive object of any gaze. If the disabled female body is "the object" of an implied male gaze, in other words, this gaze is resisted by the very "object" itself: Youssef is as much a spectacle himself as a spectator. In addition to revealing the complex subject/object dynamics at play in the execution of the work, however, the painting also articulates the mute pain that plagues Fadia throughout the whole process. It is almost as if Youssef guesses that his subject is struggling to "silence and hide" her physical pain, Fadia confesses, a pain that is heightened by the rigid and immobile pose she is forced to adopt for her painter (Daoud 2003, 81).

Just as Fadia compares herself to her daughter in the making of Jihan's film, so she cannot help but contrast her own sexual appeal in Youssef's painting with that of other women he has painted. She admits: "I did not suggest the sexual desire that was reflected in the woman of his other painting . . . and nothing of what I saw could possibly arouse a man" (Daoud 2003, 82). To borrow a phrase from Nead, Fadia effectively assumes the role of both "viewed object and viewing subject, forming and judging her image against cultural ideals" (2007, 10). Yet, poignantly, she can only find her own body wanting when measured against such ideals. If Fadia remains enthralled by a cultural ideal of female beauty that she cannot meet, Youssef's painting—like Jihan's film—is much less ready to submit to such images of female perfection: it is engaged in what we might almost call the deconstruction of this "artistic and bodily protocol" (Nead 2007, 61). In his insistence upon painting her again and again, and on constantly highlighting her scars and the awkward reflexes of her limp leg, Youssef's paintings of Fadia are not only "transgressive and disruptive" (to recall Nead's remarks on representations of the nude more generally) but make "visible new definitions of physical identity" (2007, 77).

Perhaps Youssef's last and greatest act of aesthetic deconstruction occurs when he sells all his paintings of Fadia, thus allowing her naked image to be exhibited on the walls of total strangers. "It felt like I was scattered naked in houses I did not know," Fadia recalls (Daoud 2003, 105). However, Youssef's gesture is less an invasion of Fadia's cherished privacy than a liberation of the disabled body from the social and cultural zone of exclusion that has been imposed upon it. What was once hidden from plain sight is now permanently on view. To draw on John Berger's history of representations of the nude in Europe, the naked body—even, presumably, the naked disabled body—comes to epitomize a body purged of social, cultural, or semiotic inscription (1972, 54–57). If the completed paintings of Fadia are displayed in the homes of strangers, though, it is also revealing that Youssef gives the last, unfinished one to Fadia herself who places it in her own private bedroom. For Fadia, this image is different from all the others because Youssef has erased all physical traces of her disability: it depicts neither the scar that made her "distinct and worthy" of being painted in the first place (Daoud 2003, 106) nor her physical lack of balance. In Fadia's account, the painting is as much a record of Youssef's own body—and his own intimate desires—as it is of hers. She claims that Youssef "had wanted to show her without her flaws" and "in the way he wanted her to be" (Daoud 2003, 107).

The perfect image that stares back at Fadia from her bedroom wall reflects not merely herself but Youssef as well: "In that one body of mine I do not exist alone. We are two, me and him, dividing and sharing it." Fadia can see herself and Youssef "together in this drawing . . . showing us as if we were doing what we used to do many times" (Daoud 2003, 110). Youssef's depiction of the acts of intimacy that took place between him and Fadia has the effect of restoring to his female subject the sexuality that was almost destroyed by the explosion. By watching herself in the painting and detecting the artist's desire for her body, Fadia feels herself a woman rather than a disabled body or, better, the disabled body itself becomes transformed into a site of desire. If it could be argued that the sexual body depicted in the final painting is ultimately the artist's own erotic fantasy, it remains the case that the artist's gaze fills Fadia with—a real or illusory—sexual self-confidence. In the experience of seeing herself being seen as an object of desire, Fadia becomes desirable in her own eyes. But this moment of self-recognition is, as we will see, merely the beginning of her recovery of feminine agency.

This complex series of meditations upon the power of the male gaze—whether cinematic, painterly, or literary—reveals that Daoud's *Makyaj Khafif* is a self-conscious deconstruction of the larger politics of representation that dominate the female suffering body in Arabic literature. It is Daoud's intention not merely to make the female body "visible" for the first time but to draw attention to the technologies of surveillance that have policed it for so long. Accordingly, the novel deploys what Helena Michie calls a "meta-trope of framing"—of frames and frames within frames—to lay bare the mechanisms of representation that capture Fadia's body.[5] To put it another way, Daoud exposes how Fadia remains caught between two separate and competing acts of framing: between Jihan and Youssef, between film and paint, between the cinematic chronicle of her passage from youth and beauty to disability and trauma, on the one hand, and the voyeuristic depiction of her disabled body on canvas on the other. Yet, if both framing devices serve to provide her with an instant self-image during her social "infancy" as a disabled woman—an imaginary completion, in Lacanian terms, to compensate for her (quite literal) *corps morcelé* (fragmented body)(Lacan 2004, 1–8; Michie 1989, 202)—it is clear that this seductive "completion" is not enough. For Daoud, it is only when Fadia begins to quietly resist the male gaze that she begins to constitute her own subjectivity. If Fadia is complicit in her own framing during the

5. In her book *The Flesh Made Word: Female Figures and Women's Bodies,* Michie discuses meta-tropes of female framing and unframing in the context of Victorian literature (1987, 102–23). I find her observations particularly applicable to Daoud's novel.

first half of the novel—Jihan and Youssef's gaze become the principal means through which she sees herself—the conclusion of *Makyaj Khafif* shows her defying these framing processes by refusing to take part in Jihan's film or to pose for Youssef. When at the end of the novel Fadia proclaims she "had to go from there, where everyone was meeting, and never return," she is definitively retreating from the male eyes, frames, and gazes that have dominated her life (Daoud 2003, 166). In concluding with the retreat into invisibility of its disabled protagonist, *Makyaj Khafif* re-enacts the fate of the female suffering body in Arabic literature, but with one powerful difference: Fadia's withdrawal into invisibility is the free choice of a woman wishing to define herself, rather than be defined by others, to frame herself, rather than to be framed.

Intimate Resistance

Betool Khedairi: *Ghayib*

Like *Makyaj Khafif,* Khedairi's *Ghayib* (Absent) represents a significant shift in the representation of female physical illness in Arabic literature of the Levant. Published in 2004, it is one of the few novels to focus upon the lives and experiences of the Iraqi people during the turbulent period from the rise of Saddam Hussein, through the first Gulf War of 1991, and the subsequent period of international sanctions, all the way up to the second Gulf War of 2003. It is also one of the very few works to reveal the shifting gender balance in modern Iraqi society and the traumatic effect of the last thirty years upon Iraqi masculinity.[6] Nevertheless, the novel's importance for this study lies in its depiction of the disability of its first-person female narrator/protagonist, Dalal, and the illness of another female character, Ilham. In its representation of these two bodies, *Absent* again expands the repertoire of the female suffering body in contemporary Arabic literature.

It is through the voice of its female protagonist Dalal that the events of the novel are narrated. She relates—in a mixture of realism and black comedy—the daily life of the occupants of a building in the heart of

6. For an excellent study of contemporary Arab women's writers see Valassopoulos (2007).

Baghdad as they seek to cope with political oppression, social and economic deprivation, and endless reports of violence and death. Dalal's narrative focuses on the female occupants who constantly seek refuge in a fortune-teller to help them make sense of the various emotional, physical, and social problems that assail them. They rush to the fortune-teller to help them find a cure for the loneliness they experience at night, to pour their heart out over their inability to escape the country, to rage at their deteriorating health, and to bemoan the ever-decreasing number of men available to support and take care of them. In the context of this study, however, it is Dalal's own facial disfigurement and Ilhan's breast cancer that are most significant.

To be sure, Khedairi's novel is something of an anatomy of the suffering body: it is filled with images of mutilated, wounded, scarred, and withered corporeality.

At the same time, the traumatized physical body is intimately related to the traumatized social and political body of Iraq: "[B]odily processes outfold" into culture, to borrow a phrase from Arthur and Joan Kleinman, while "culture infolds into the body" (1994, 710–11). Yet, *Absent* moves decisively beyond the discursive regime that transforms physical disability into a crude metaphor for the plight of the nation state. For Khedairi, just as for Daoud, the female suffering body is more than merely a signifier for some prior and apparently more urgent social trauma. In fact, what is remarkable about Dalal and Ilham's illness narratives is the extent to which they preserve the *particularity* of their respective traumas —facial disfigurement and breast cancer—in the face of external forces.

After a blood clot on the brain at the age of 12, Dalal's face is left disfigured: her mouth is "crooked" and her lips "drawn across to the right side of [her] face as though someone were pulling them with an invisible thread" (Khedairi 2005, 12). She recounts how the face that stares back at her in the mirror causes her to cry: "I tried to convince myself that I was normal. My sad attempts to whistle always failed. I'd cry in front of the mirror that echoed back the sound *phht, phht* instead of a long elegant whistle" (Khedairi 2005, 12). Yet, even this moment of visual trauma is denied her by a power outage that leaves the building in darkness: the protagonist is no longer able to see her image anywhere. For the reader of *Absent*, Dalal's personal illness narrative is similarly occluded by her stories of other people's lives and pain amidst the chaos of war-torn Iraq. In the interstices of her different stories, however, we can find and begin to reconstruct the story of her own illness.

During the course of the novel, Dalal's own illness narrative thus emerges slowly and obliquely. It is rarely expressed directly, but rather negatively, in a moment of reaction, defensiveness, or self-consciousness. She notices, for example, when others stare at her misshapen lips and even tells her hairdresser friend that no man would ever be interested in a woman who has her problem (Khedairi 2005, 150). When this same friend tries to correct her appearance with makeup, Dalal rejects the new shape insisting "it's been painted on . . . it's a fake" (Khedairi 2005, 107). For Dalal, as we have seen, her inability to confront her own disfigurement leads her to immerse herself in the suffering of others: "Before the sanctions started, I used to feel that my life was divided into two halves, the time before the stroke and what came after it. Nowadays everyone talks about the Days of Plenty, and the times that followed; the days before the war, and those that followed; life before the crisis, and after it. I, too, find myself, reluctantly, thinking like everyone else" (Khedairi 2005, 105). If her facial disfigurement was the "primal scene" or event in her life,[7] though, Dalal can only articulate this personal trauma through the collective trauma that is everyday life in Baghdad. The character who most embodies this collective trauma is her friend Ilham.

To Dalal, Ilham's acute illness is intimately and concretely connected to the sickness of the political body of Iraq. After discovering that she has advanced breast cancer, Ilham immediately blames it upon the social deprivation that she is forced to endure. Rather than bemoaning a seemingly arbitrary punishment—"why me?"—she sees her illness as the belated arrival of a collective fate. When revealing the "red swelling on her right breast" to Dalal, for instance, Ilham announces "it seems that it's

7. The term "primal scene" was first introduced by Sigmund Freud in his reference to painful events in one's childhood that later become the cause of psychological and emotional traumas. See Freud (1963, 213–34).

my turn now," adding that she "has seen it often enough to tell the difference" (Khedairi 2005, 80). For Ilham, her illness is the inevitable consequence of the economic sanctions imposed by the West after the 1991 Gulf War: "We're the real targets." The "we" here refers to the "women and children" who Ilham sees on a daily basis in her capacity as a nurse: "The hospital I work for is full of sick women and babies dying in their mother's arms" (Khedairi 2005, 58). By the same logic, Ilham attributes her disease to the shifting gender balance in the nation following the disappearance and death of a large number of Iraqi men since the onset of the Iran/Iraq and Gulf Wars. In fact, she muses that "what has happened wouldn't have happened" if only she had a man: "I didn't feel the lump while it was growing. It continued to enlarge while I was preoccupied with my work. It never occurred to me to examine my body looking for a tumour . . . that's the benefit of having a man" (Khedairi 2005, 81).

Despite her grave physical condition, Ilham appears more concerned about her job than her illness. As she makes clear to Dalal, she cannot even pay for her treatment without continuing to work as a nurse. When she undergoes a mastectomy, she worries in case her colleagues at the hospital will realize she has been seriously ill and put her job in jeopardy (Khedairi 2005, 122). To support her, the other residents perform small but significant acts of charity: Umm Ghayib, who is Dalal's aunt, designs an artificial breast for Ilham made from a "mixture of beeswax, sawdust and tiny cut-offs of nylon," which she "molds . . . into a moderate-sized dome" and then "sews a bra with double lining" (Khedairi 2005, 122). In the same way, the hairdresser sends Ilham a "wig that was a replica of her hair and a set of false eyelashes," Abou Ghayib donates money for her painkillers, while the fortune-teller sends her a secret remedy to "heal [her] wound and regulate the period" (Khedairi 2005, 121).

Such small acts of solidarity transform the female suffering body from a private space, endured in secret, to a public one, acknowledged and supported by one and all. To be sure, Ilham's illness remains grounded in the particularity of her physical symptoms at all times: it is never permitted to become a corporeal metaphor or allegory for some larger and more urgent social sickness. Nevertheless, her suffering is transformed from "the bottom up," so to speak, into a social experience that touches the lives of everyone in the building. Everyone is able to share in her pain because of their own physical and emotional traumas. For Khedairi, female physical illness moves out of the solitary bedroom in which it had been marginalized and comes to embody the building as a whole and the community who share it. If Ilham's illness narrative becomes a means of affirming the quiet stoicism of the Iraqi people, though, Khedairi's vision is ultimately too pessimistic to take refuge in such consolations: Ilham's story is cut short halfway through the story "not because she has died of cancer, but because she has been imprisoned" by the Iraqi intelligence services (Khedairi 2005, 131).[8] In this way, too, Ilham's illness narrative is at one and the same time a political narrative: her disappearance is not a natural consequence of her disease, but the political decision of her country's regime.

However, after Ilham's body is erased by hidden political forces, Dalal's illness/disability narrative continues to develop through her relationship with Adil, an undercover government spy.[9] It is the growing attraction between Dalal and Adil that reconstitutes the former's disfigurement as a site of desire rather than repulsion. At the same time, this relationship is (just as we saw in the case of Daoud's *Makyaj Khafif*) a complex and ambiguous melange of surveillance, mirror-play, and eroticism. For Adil, it is precisely the lack of "femininity" he finds in Dalal that is most appealing about her: he is "so used to dealing with people who have a disfigurement" that there is nothing strange in his attraction to her (Khedairi 2005, 151). In contrast to more conventionally beautiful women, Dalal does not constitute an erotic threat to him: "[A] beautiful woman smells of danger. I don't like it when someone tosses me a piece of creamy cake. I could slip, or it might be a trap" (Khedairi 2005, 160). Just as in the case of Fadia from *Makyaj Khafif*, Dalal's disfigurement is thus reconstituted erotically under the male gaze. During one physical encounter, Adil leads her to the bedroom, lays her down on the bed, and removes the scarf that is covering her

8. The allegation behind her imprisonment is that Ilham had been selling human organs to her boyfriend which she took from the operating room at the hospital where she worked.

9. Adil pretends he is a physiotherapist who helps install false limbs for those who need them (Khedairi 2005, 137).

face. The lover then lights a candle to illuminate the darkened room and asks her to observe herself in a mirror. When she follows Adil's bidding, he whispers to her to "imagine that [her] lips are about to take flight" and that "her mouth was being caressed by the wind" (Khedairi 2005, 163), all the while claiming she was like "silver stars" that had "to be rubbed so that [she] may shine" (Khedairi 2005, 165). In this experience of seeing herself being seen by her lover, Dalal (like Fadia before her) begins to re-identify with her own body as a possible locus of desire.

If *Absent* recapitulates the dynamics of the gaze we first identified in Daoud's novel, though, it also adds a significant new element to the mix: tactility. It is important to note that, while gazing at Dalal gazing at herself, Adil massages her feet. As a consequence, the disfigured body is transformed from an image to be contemplated into a tactile reality to be experienced. To embodiment theorist Elizabeth Grosz, what is called the haptic dimension of experience undercuts the traditional subject-object dualism of the optic:

> The epistemological value of sight is based on the clarity and precision of the images of which it is composed. An image, traditionally has three characteristics: it presents a manifold field or set of events in terms of simultaneity (it is the only non-temporal or synchronous sense); it functions at a distance, setting up a space or field between the seer and the seen, the physical and the psychical; and it does not imply or presume causality (because the other senses are momentary and occasioned by events, vision is ongoing and need not be focused on or caused by any object). (1994, 97)

While sight allows for the "raw elements, the data necessary for the production of knowledge" (1994, 97), Grosz argues that touch "defines a more corporeal 'atmosphere'—more fundamental because literally closer to the body—in which the visual experience of the world and other bodies must be contextualized" (Punday 2003, 75–77). For Grosz, skin, in particular, is "the ground for the articulation of orifices, erotogenic rims, cuts on the body's surface, loci of exchange between the inside and the outside, points of conversion of the outside into the body, and of the inside out of the body" (1994, 36). The experience of tactility, in short, "defines the context in which all other relations between the body and the world, and objects within the world must be understood" (Punday 2003, 76). This radical corporeality arguably short-circuits the discursivity that had objectified the female suffering body in Arabic literature: female physical illness and disability in *Absent* are no longer simply an image in the eye of a male beholder but a non-reducible, fleshly presence. By touching every part of her body, Adil affirms Dalal's visibility and presence as an affecting and affected being rather than a maimed woman. In a word, he encounters her body in all its materiality rather than merely an idea of that body.

Perhaps we must qualify this claim by adding that Dalal's new erotic self-image remains (just as in the case of Fadia before her) heavily mediated by her male lover's gaze. It must also be borne in mind that Adil's interest in Dalal is triggered by his covert position as an agent of the state. Accordingly, his erotic gaze is imbued with the politics of surveillance and discipline: we might see their relationship as a powerful dramatization of Foucault's famous claim that "power seeps into the very grain of individuals, reaches right into their bodies, permeates their gestures, what they say, how they learn to live and work with other people" (quoted in Sheridan 1980, 217). For Khedairi, in other words, Dalal's body not only transmits the story of her disfigurement but also begins to tell the truth about the nature of the state to which she belongs. In her physical encounter with Adil, Dalal affirms the truth that the gaze of the state is truly panoptical.

For Khedairi, however, it is also clear that Dalal resists Adil's attempts to survey and discipline her body. By allowing Dalal to reclaim her erotic identity, Adil even opens up the possibility of resistance against someone who is, after all, a representative of the oppressive regime under which she has suffered. The visual and tactile signs of Adil's desire—his soft touch probing her body through the opening in her shirt, his hand slipping downward to places that have always been kept hidden, and his eyes as they meet Dalal's in a moment of full passion—all give Dalal power over a man who, in every other way, has power over her. In the midst of his attempt to control her, Adil unwittingly finds himself rendered powerless by his genuine attraction, and even love, for this disabled woman.

In the end of the narrative, then, we encounter a very different Dalal from the reticent storyteller at the beginning: she is now an agent of potential social resistance. It is possible to see the outline of this resistance taking shape when Dalal decides to find out what lies behind the walls of the tennis court near their building—a territory marked off as a forbidden zone (Khedairi 2005, 190–94).[10] At the end of the novel, we also find her deciding to teach a young newspaper boy how to read and write. Symbolically passing on her own role as narrator to the young boy—a child who is one of the few males in the novel—Dalal seeks, in her own small way, to rebuild the shattered physical and political body of Baghdad. If *Absent* undoubtedly re-invokes the classic gesture of depicting the disabled woman as a metaphor for the nation (see chapter 2), then, it simultaneously transforms that trope: the female suffering body is stripped of its passivity and invested with a new and urgent sense of voice and agency. By permitting the sick/disabled woman to speak for herself and in her own voice, she ceases to become merely a passive *tabula rasa* ripe for textual inscription and, instead, becomes the fully realized and embodied mouthpiece for herself and her community.

Passage to Subjectivity

Haifa' Bitar: *Imra'a min Hadha al-'Asr*

Finally, let us turn to another recent depiction of physical illness and disability by a controversial female writer. Haifa' Bitar's work repeatedly seeks to offer an insight into the gritty reality of women's lives in the Arab world—their loves, desires, aspirations, and fears. Her novels and short stories focus on tragic female characters who suffer social and psychological injury either at the hands of men or because of their own misplaced ideals and aspirations. In *Imra'a min Hadha al-'Asr* (A Woman of This Modern Age, 2004),[11] Bitar tells the story of Maryam, a modern woman whose confessional narrative recounts her experience with breast cancer against the backdrop of two failed marriages and a series of destructive relationships with men.

10. Dalal discovers that the place is filled with masses of dead bodies that have not even been buried.

11. I will refer throughout to the novel in the abbreviated form *Imra'a*.

To be sure, the book is principally a self-reflective narrative on illness, but (like the rest of Bitar's work) it has provoked widespread criticism for its explicit depiction of "taboo" subjects such as female sexuality. On the one hand, the novel is a meditation on Maryam's experience with breast cancer, mastectomy, and aggressive medical treatment. On the other, the sub-narrative makes it also the story of its narrator's quest for freedom and a challenge to the status quo's monopoly upon female sexuality in some Arab cultures. In short, *Imra'a* intertwines illness and sexuality to offer what Elizabeth Alexander elsewhere calls "a map of lived experience and a way of printing suffering as well as joy upon the flesh" (1994, 691).[12]

It is clear that Bitar is deeply concerned with the corporeality of her protagonist's illness from the first visible signs of symptoms to the traumas of surgery, chemotherapy, and radiation treatment. As she grapples with the discovery that she has breast cancer, Maryam offers the reader an intimate map of the physical landscape of her body by giving detailed descriptions of the phenomenological disorientation her illness produces. Like so many other illness narratives, she describes a process of alienation from her pre-illness, healthy, and sexually desirable body. In the period immediately before her mastectomy, Maryam feels her breast under the shower for the last time then tells how she bid it adieu and "stored its feel and constitution in the palm of her hand" (2004, 19).[13]

As she tenderly feels her breast, she recalls "the palms of all the men who caressed" it. She then whispers to her "poor breast," reminding it that "when you were healthy and strong they used to rush to you but now that you are sick no one stands by you and you remain alone" (Bitar 2004, 19). For Maryam, her physical sense of well-being is deeply tied to her sexuality. In the scene where she confronts the reality of losing her breast, it is clear that she sees it as the annihilation of her sexual identity and all

12. Alexander is here speaking in the context of a discussion of Audre Lorde's experience with breast cancer as it is narrated in the latter's work. In both Lorde's autobiographical narrative and Bitar's fictional equivalent, however, we can detect parallel patterns of speaking of the body.

13. All quotations from the novel are my translation. At the time of the writing of this chapter, the English translation had not appeared.

that it entailed: "The end of my breast is the end of men [man] in my life," adding that she "could not after today love a man when I had one breast" only (Bitar 2004, 15).

When the mastectomy is performed, Maryam's main concern becomes what has happened to her lost breast. She asks the nurse: "Where do you throw cancerous breasts?" then thinks that "amputated breasts should be buried in a manner that befits them because breasts are a symbol of life and tenderness and beauty" (Bitar 2004, 22). The sight of her "new body" with the "red, scarred skin" (Bitar 2004, 24) makes her want to "flee the prison of the body" (Bitar 2004, 30). Indeed, the trauma of her body is so real and present that Maryam is led to mourn the loss of her removed breast in almost religious terms: "I don't know why I felt the need for a divine justice, a justice that would save me from the feeling of abyss into which I was slipping" (Bitar 2004, 24).

Yet, despite or because of her trauma, Maryam offers a compelling narrative of the devastation that illness wreaks upon her body. To the cancer victim, it seems that her entire body is beginning to break up both physically and psychologically. Maryam feels a sense of radical disconnection not merely between the different parts of her body but between her body and her sense of self. As she undergoes her first chemotherapy treatment, Maryam describes how the medicine dripping through the syringe left her wanting to "collect her self that was scattered across the place" (Bitar 2004, 50). By the same logic, this sense of physical fragmentation soon leads to a linguistic fragmentation: "I discovered that I have lost the fluency of clause. My sentences are disconnected and my phrases are broken and I feel gaps of forgetfulness in the heart of my brain" (Bitar 2004, 100). Such moments of linguistic breakdown testify to what Scarry famously calls the inexpressibility of the body in pain. For Scarry, pain is "language destroying: as the content of one's world disintegrates, so the content of one's language disintegrates: as the self disintegrates, so that which would express and project the self is robbed of its source and its subject." In Maryam's case, more precisely, the body in pain is experienced spatially as "the contraction of the universe down to the immediate vicinity of the body" (1985, 35). There is no longer any world to refer to outside that of her own trauma.

Like so many of the female protagonists we have encountered in this chapter, Maryam's response to the physical and linguistic fragmentation produced by her illness is to seek to write and talk her way back to wholeness. It is by writing a history of the female suffering body that this body can begin to be put back together. At every treatment session, Maryam embarks on a journey across time where she recalls her past relationships with men, her traumatic experience of motherhood, and her lost hopes and aspirations. In each case, her reminiscences are less an exercise in consolatory nostalgia than an attempt to symbolically heal the wound between her pre- and post-illness selves: Maryam seeks to recapture "the taste of the past" but always recognizes that this past has taken on "a new flavor and new perspective, the perspective of a woman who had cancer . . ." (Bitar 2004, 30). This passage highlights what feminist theorist Jackie Stacey, in her *Teratologies: A Cultural Study of Cancer*, describes as the complex relationship between female subjectivity, identity construction, and the cancer experience whereby the body—in the face of cancer and amputation—"tells a new story and so demands a reinterpretation of recent life history" (1997, 5).

For Maryam, then, her illness narrative becomes a dialogue between her present ill body and her previous healthy one. It is also a dialogue between her self and her body and between the different parts of her body. As such, Maryam's narrative transforms her female suffering body into what Alexander would call a "collage" that is "overlapping and discernibly dialogic" (1994, 697). To put it in Maryam's own words: "I am outside the parameters of life and try to create an intimate dialogue with myself to boost my morals . . ." (Bitar 2004, 100). Likewise, her narrative intimately intertwines the medical and the affective, the body of the patient and the body of the child, lover, and mother. The memories she narrates are randomly sparked off by the contingent circumstances of each treatment session: her first chemotherapy session, for instance, leads her to recall a lover who was every bit as "difficult and repulsive" as chemotherapy (Bitar 2004, 50). When she begins to experience the side effects of chemotherapy and to feel that her body is being abused by the cancer, she begins to tell of her abuse (and the abuse of others) of her sexuality. Such narratives are not merely personal either but social and political.

Maryam particularly reflects upon the cruelties that befall women, be it from a repressive husband who turned her "from a lover to a slave" (Bitar 2004, 70), a cruel mother-in-law who stripped her of her husband and son, or exploitive lovers who made her feel "as if [she] was being raped" (Bitar 2004, 48). If Maryam's illness becomes the basis for a personal and social autobiography, though, it is not merely a story of her victimhood. Bitar describes her protagonist's sexuality in an almost unprecedentedly graphic manner for an Arab woman writer. This is, after all, a protagonist who freely confesses that "the fever of desire" (Bitar 2004, 102) cannot be restrained by "the glory of virtue that had a rotten smell" (Bitar 2004, 96), but only through an explicit invitation to a stranger to "have sex with her" (Bitar 2004, 98).

The protagonist's confrontation with chronic illness and possible death here produces what Mary K. Deshazer calls "the erotic power and expressions of desire" by women with fatal illnesses (2005, 173). In her study of women's representation in cancer literature in Western culture, Deshazer notes that a number of these writings highlight the ways in which the experience of chronic illness produces an "intense eroticism" whereby the female cancer patient explores her sexuality "through the disruptive lens of terminal cancer" (2005, 174). For Maryam, the threat of losing her sexuality through illness drives her to explore her sexuality freely and intricately. By repeatedly reminding the reader of her lived bodily experience in health and illness, Maryam thus "works towards the [scarred] body's integration through struggle, a synecdoche for the struggle of the self to remain whole" or reconstruct a wholeness (Alexander 1994, 709).

Perhaps the most intriguing aspect of Maryam's unfolding illness narrative, though, is that it increasingly serves to undermine the image of her pre-illness, "healthy" self. To be more precise, it becomes clear that, long before her illness ever struck, Maryam's self was *already* in crisis due to the suffocating societal expectations placed upon her: marriage, motherhood, career aspirations. Far from recuperating a lost "wholeness," then, Maryam's illness narrative reveals the extent to which her subjectivity was denied her *before* her illness. If critics such as Scarry rightly emphasize that the body in pain frequently serves to destroy subjectivity,

Bitar's narrative turns this logic on its head: it is only through illness that Maryam becomes a subject in the first place.

For Maryam, to adopt a phrase from Bruno Latour (1993), it seems that "she has never been a subject at all": her right to identity has consistently been foreclosed by the social norms she has been forced to live by. From a husband who imposed a specific dress code and social mannerisms upon her, to lovers who dictated how she behaved and performed, Maryam has endured what Bryan Turner calls the "loss of sensuous ownership of the body," and a "form of corporeal alienation." This has produced a "commodification of [her] sexuality devoid of subjective commitment and affective attachment" (1996, 220). Even her insatiable sexual desire is merely the inverse sign of the sense of lack, denial, and repression that invades every other aspect of her life.

In this sense, Maryam's illness trauma does not so much result in the deconstruction of her prior subjectivity but, in a term coined by Bibi Bakare Yusuf, the "desubjectification of a desubjectified subject" (1999, 319).

If Maryam's illness initially causes further bodily alienation, though, it ultimately forces her to re-examine her world and to gain a heightened "self-reflective vision" of things. It is only through illness, paradoxically, that she begins to experience subjective consciousness without the prohibition of external forces and individuals. According to Kleinman's account of chronic illness, "insight can be the result of an often grim, though occasionally, luminous, lived wisdom of the body in pain and the mind troubled" (1988, 55), and Maryam undergoes a similar transformation in perception. For Maryam, illness allows her to reclaim a self that had been lost to men: she is no longer "concerned with the world of men," and this gives her "a true sense of security" (Bitar 2004, 122). The only man who remains the focus of her life is her son, who makes her "forget that she is without a breast" and thus takes away the feeling of being diseased and scarred (Bitar 2004, 153). Such an act of self-exemption from the world of men is complemented by a growing sense of solidarity with women who have experienced the same kind of trauma. Maryam confesses that she wants to experiment with "the treatment of love" on women whose breasts, like hers, have been struck with cancer and removed (Bitar 2004, 213). In the end, it is this "female-identified experience" that provides meaning for her life after the illness, the treatment, and the remission period.

In Bitar's *Imra'a,* then, we encounter another powerful attempt by an Arab woman writer to reclaim the female suffering body: whereas previous Arabic narratives of physical illness focused on the ill figure "as-she-is-written" about, Bitar's narrative depicts the sick protagonist "as-she-writes"[14] her body and self into existence. To be sure, Maryam's illness narrative remains characterized by an acute sense of pain—a pain that permeates not only her body but, as we have seen, pervades her sense of self-identity and esteem. It is a pain that, in Kleinman's theory on illness narratives, becomes the central "idiom of a network of communication and negotiation" between her body, her self, and wider social and cultural values (1988, 72). Accordingly, what is unique about Maryam's own attempt to put her subjectivity back together is that it does not depend solely on what Grosz calls "categories of interiority" but rather upon the "primacy of corporeality" (1994, viii). For Maryam, the corporeal space that is the ill body becomes the site where affect, psychology, and social values all play out: it involves both surface and depth, materiality and interiority. Such a multi-layered corporeal space does not merely enable her to speak the body in pain, but the sexual body, the social body, and the body politic. The aggressive and traumatic suffering of her body makes her aware of her corporeality for almost the first time in her life and initiates her into her journey of self-discovery. This journey culminates in a freedom from the destructive control and domination of men, on the one hand, and a freedom to construct new relationships with her son and with other cancer-stricken women, on the other: "My happiness is no longer connected to an other" (Bitar 2004, 177), she admits, adding that "it is as if this illness has made deeper and stronger roots for me in the landscape of life." In the final pages of the book, Maryam feels that she has "crossed from one border to another" (Bitar 2004, 172), and *Imra'a* is indeed the story

14. For a detailed discussion of figures being written about and those who write see Susan Rubin Suleiman (1985, 352–77).

of how the experience of illness paradoxically produces a new, psychically and socially more secure, subjectivity.

The Visible Body

In the three texts discussed in this closing chapter—*Makyaj Khafif li-Hadhih al-Layla, Ghayib* (Absent), and *Imra'a min Hadha al-'Asr*—we see the ill female body entering into narrative visibility. It is with contemporary Arab writers such as Daoud, Khedairi, and Bitar that female physical illness and disability begins to be written into existence and given access to its own subjectivity, structures of feeling, and imaginative life world. As they disrupt the traditional representational mode of speaking and writing about this ill body, the three writers in question contribute—each in their own way—to creating a new narrative discourse. For Daoud, Khedairi, and Bitar, the female suffering body is neither perceived as a pure lack or deficiency of womanhood, nor as a metaphor for some wider social malaise, nor as the victim of a patriarchal taboo and shame, but is located at the very center of contemporary Arabic fiction.

To begin with, we saw how Daoud's *Makyaj Khafif* breaks decisively with the prevailing regime of representing female physical illness and disability by allowing the female suffering body to represent itself.

Unlike Daoud's earlier novels—where bodily ailment and injury often served as symbols of ruin, destruction, and war—*Makyaj Khafif* divests the female disabled body of metaphoric meaning as it writes out the corporeal reality of its disability. It is true, of course, that Fadia's disability is caused by a bomb explosion but, as Moroccan writer and critic Muhammad Berada emphasizes, "the novel does not evoke the [Lebanese Civil] War nor does it imprison itself inside of it" (Adabwafan.com). According to Fatima al-Muhsin, such a reading would destroy the novel's unique temperament and mood (2005). Rather, it is the female disabled body itself that slowly becomes the novel's object of focus, lending it a physical and embodied presence that had otherwise been obscured. By focusing on the materiality of physical pain, Daoud opens up new fields of knowledge from which to grasp the lived experience of female physical disability. In order to achieve this material intimacy, Daoud employs a highly specific narrative strategy—the meta-trope of framing—to anatomize what Foucault famously identified as the "space through which bodies and eyes meet" (Foucault 1993, xi).

It is the cinematic and artistic framing of Fadia that allow her body to become an object for the narrative gaze.[15] As we saw, the framing process enables the protagonist to confront the reality of her physicality, and even to come to terms with her physical lack, all the while constructing her material visibility for the reader. To start with, Fadia's own first-person narrative is clearly mediated through her male admirers: her own point of view is merely a supplement to the point of view of the gazer. Yet, this same gaze, which at the outset affects the authorial quality of Fadia's voice, also opens up the possibility of resistance to it. When Fadia begins to thwart the cinematic and artistic gaze, her own subjective voice and identity emerge for the first time in the novel. In this way, *Makyaj Khafif* not only chronicles the moment when the female suffering body enters into narrative discourse but also the process through which the self begins to search for its own subjectivity and the subjectivity of other female bodies in pain.

As we saw in the second section of this chapter, Khedairi's *Ghayib* (Absent) contributes to what we might call this growing "corporeal turn" in representations of female physical illness and disability. To be sure, Khedairi's novel reactivates the old trope by which female illness is related to the sickness of the Iraqi nation state but—unlike previous examples of this genre—it does not sacrifice the particular materiality of lives of pain. It testifies to this materiality by bringing it into sight for the first time: Ilham, for example, shows Dalal the marks of the disease on her body. Yet, the suffering body of Ilham to which Dalal bears witness is soon erased from the space of the narrative by the oppressive measures of the state; the dynamics of vision that accompany Dalal's own illness narrative are more complex. For Khedairi, the voyeuristic gaze of Adil, Dalal's lover, is at one and the same time the political gaze of a surveillance state

15. For a discussion of the dynamics of the gaze, objects, and fields of vision in arts and narrative see Peter Brooks (1993).

upon its most vulnerable subjects. Adil "deploys a gaze subtended by the desire to know," to borrow an expression from Peter Brooks, "a gaze that wants both to record the observable and to penetrate to the essential, to appropriate both appearances and their inner principles" (1993, 89).[16] In Brooks's terms, Adil's erotico-political gaze strips down Dalal's body in order to rebuild it in its own image: the female suffering body "ente[rs] the machinery of power" to which Adil belongs and is powerless to resist as he "breaks it down and rearranges it" (1993, 138).

Yet, Adil's visual power over Dalal is counteracted by her own tactile mode of resistance. It is here that Khedairi's text moves beyond the dynamics of the gaze with which representations of female illness and disability have so long been concerned: the erotic encounter between Dalal and Adil captures the transition of ill and disabled bodies from objects of vision to affective, desiring economies. For Khedairi, Dalal's tactile power over Adil repels his visual power over her and opens up a new sphere of erotico-political resistance. When Dalal gains erotic power over Adil, it is no coincidence that she also gains the agency to participate in acts of social resistance against the very state which Adil embodies. The social and political defiance that Dalal represents at the end of the novel is not the only signifier of the agency that her disfigured body begins to gain in the narrative, because, as Khedairi's "primary spectator" and narrator, Dalal is the textual lens through which we view the individual and collective suffering in Iraq.[17] In *Absent*, then, female illness and disability is not so much a passive metaphor by which male authors may represent the collective sickness of the Iraqi body politic as the other way around: it is only through the corporeality of Dalal's personal illness narrative that the wider political narrative itself can be represented.

For me, the corporeal turn in female illness narratives gains full momentum in Bitar's *Imra'a*. It represents yet another development in the

16. If an erotic dynamic was also underway in Daoud's novel, in Khedairi's work this voyeurism is described in detail, hence giving it more importance in relation to the visibility of the protagonist.

17. For a detailed discussion of primary spectators see Jean Gallagher (1998).

narrative strategies through which the story of the female suffering body is transmitted. As our discussion of the novel revealed, Bitar is not simply interested in making visible ill female bodies through sensory capacities such as seeing and touching but in allowing this body to participate in the production of knowledge about itself and its suffering. To Bitar, it is physical pain itself that enables Maryam to become a full subject for the first time in her life. Maryam's cancer narrative finds her establishing a dialogic relationship between her body and self, between her past and present sexuality, and between her once healthy and currently ill body. Such a narrative creates what Kleinman calls "a unique texture of meaning—external layers written over internal ones to form a palimpsest" of her own experience with breast cancer (1988, 32). In *Imra'a*, the reader bears witness to a woman's journey from a healthy, yet socially repressed, life to a liberated, if pain-wracked, existence which leads to a new and more positive set of relations with both women and men.

What, to conclude this chapter, is taking place in contemporary Arabic narratives of the female suffering body? It is perhaps worth concluding this chapter with a salutary *caveat lector* to anyone tempted to pronounce in general terms upon "the body." According to Nead, there is "no monolithic category of the body," rather a variety of types, some of which have been identified as "deviant" and, even worse, kept invisible and silent (2007, 64). Yet, what is still more crucial for Nead is "the defiant assertion of the autonomy of those other kinds of bodies and subjectivities" (2007, 64) that have for long been invisible. For Daoud, Khedairi, and Bitar, we might say it is the defiant assertion of these other, unwritten bodies that forms the subject of their recent fiction: they write into existence a new set of utterly singular and autonomous female bodies that defy any attempt to categorize or universalize them. They also devise new and experimental narrative strategies to open up the claustrophobically narrow narrative world of female illness. By deconstructing the politics of the gaze toward female physical illness/disability, by recuperating the lived materiality of the body in pain through tactility, and by transforming that body into a site of agency and subjectivity, Daoud, Khedairi, and Bitar break with the code of silence that has surrounded the female suffering body in Arabic literature for so long. Perhaps most simply and most powerfully, however, they allow those bodies to speak for themselves and as themselves: ill and disabled women are granted their own first-person narratives for the first time in Arabic fiction. In short, we might say that the singular achievement of Daoud, Khedairi, and Bitar is to give the female suffering body her own voice because, as Luce Irigaray famously puts it, "To find a voice (*voix*) is to find a way (*voie*)" (1985, 209).

CONCLUSION

In one of the most controversial contemporary novels by an Arab female writer, a woman falls ill and confronts the prospect of imminent death. It is not, of course, the first time a woman becomes ill in Arabic literature. As we saw in the Introduction to this book, it could even be argued that modern Arabic writing—in the form of Mahfouz's *Cairo Trilogy*—begins with the illness and death of a woman: Amina. Yet, in this modern instance, something dramatically different takes place: female illness and disability are no longer occluded by stigma nor over-burdened with symbolism. For Bitar, author of *Imra'a Min Hadha al-'Asr* (chapter 3), the female suffering body of her protagonist Maryam becomes, almost for the first time in the history of Arabic literature, a speaking, living, affective subject. This book has effectively sought to tell the story of these two sick women and of the social, cultural, and literary gulf that separates them. What, to bring this study to a close, is the difference between Amina and Maryam? How does Arabic literature move from reducing the sick/disabled female subject to silence, on the one hand, to permitting it to speak for itself on the other? And, why, finally, is the female suffering body slowly beginning to be recognized today?

An Anatomy of Female Subjectivity

In this book, I have sought to offer an aesthetic genealogy of representations of female physical illness and disability in Arabic literature from 1950 to the present. My aim has been to show that the story of representations of what I have called the female suffering body is the story of a slow passage from invisibility to visibility, from metaphoric and symbolic construction to corporeal and affective materiality, and from textual silence to speech, self-expression, and narrative. To be absolutely clear, I do not mean to imply that the ill or disabled female body is necessarily or naturally a suffering body but rather to show how a position of suffering is imposed upon women from without by a series of discourses. By the same token, I do not seek to imply that there is a "right" way to represent female illness and disability with all the normative assumptions such terms carry. If my book tells a story, it is not of the passage from a "bad" way of representing female illness/disability to a "good" one, but from a total absence of representation to a position where women are, for the first time in Arabic literature, able to represent themselves. In other words, I have sought to show how women are gaining the power to narrate their own bodies. What have been the key signs of this aesthetic and narrative transformation in representing female illness and disability?

To begin with, chapter 1, which dealt with works of male writers who published between 1950 and 2000, showed how the ill female body was rendered absent in the first place. It demonstrated how male writers expelled that body from the space of the narrative and maintained a kind of exclusion zone around it, preventing it from coming into contact with other, normalized bodies. For Arab male writers like Mahmoud Taymur, Yusuf al-Siba'i, and Naguib Mahfouz (to name but a few), the female body in pain became a kind of repressed other of the visible, highly sexualized female body that so many male narratives of the period embraced and celebrated.[1] Yet, as this chapter sought to demonstrate, the repressed other returns. In many ways, the absence of a female illness narrative in these literary texts itself speaks volumes about the level of social, cultural, and religious stigmatization which afflicted the female body in pain.

It thus became essential in this chapter to focus not on the presence of the female suffering body but rather upon her conspicuous and constitutive absence from the texts in question. As a consequence, my focus was less upon the excluded woman's corporeality than on what Foucault

1. In many male writers' work, much emphasis is placed on the sensuality and sexuality of female characters. Some of these writers include Fathi Ghanim, Mahfouz, Yusuf Idris, Jabra Ibrahim Jabra, and Mina to name but a few.

would call the discursive regime that excluded her: female physical illness and disability became a means of laying bare the discourse of normalization. For Chris Shilling, writing on embodiment in Foucault, it is precisely the corporeal body that discourse serves to erase: he argues that the "biological, physical or material body can never be grasped by the Foucauldian approach as its existence is permanently deferred behind the grids of meaning imposed by discourse." By focusing on the body as nothing more than the passive surface upon which discourse may be inscribed, Foucault and the genealogical approach he exemplifies occludes the corporeality of that body (2003, 70–71).[2] In chapter 1, I thus sought to track the privileged ways in which Arab male writers put the materiality of the female suffering body into discourse.

As we saw, the discursive function of the ill female body is to serve pre-existing and apparently more urgent social, religious, and political economies.[3] The representation of female physical illness/disability records moments in time where the characters become what Mary Poovey would describe as "objects of another's discourse" rather than "women as subjects of their own" (1990, 29). For Susan Wendell, the ill body is represented as a "cultural construction and the body or body parts are taken to be symbolic forms in a culture" (1999, 325), while the experience of the lived body itself is obliterated. By being placed in the service of a cultural construction, what is most intimate to the experience of female physical illness and disability—in short, pain—seems, in Scarry's words, "to have the remote character of some deep subterranean fact, belonging to an

2. To be sure, Shilling does not deny that Foucault's work is still concerned with the body "as a real entity," specifically in his analysis of the body in relation to scientific thought (2003, 70).

3. It is important to clarify here that, while I am critical of the tendency of male writers to represent female physical illness and disability, it would be unfair to say that these writers *intentionally* sought to erase the female suffering body. As we have seen, the majority of these texts were produced during turbulent periods of social and political change—together with deep-seated opposition to such change—and thus it is inevitable that their responses should be ambivalent. In the end, though, the result is the same whether intentional or not: the female physical body suffering illness/disability was indeed occluded.

invisible geography that, however portentous, has no reality because it has not yet manifested itself on the visible surface of the earth" (1985, 3).

To be sure, this book could be accused of being complicit in what Scarry calls the process of rendering the female body in pain remote, invisible, subterranean. It is true that my own analyses of female illness and disability in chapter 1 read the suffering body discursively as the site of various social, political, and religious regimes of power/knowledge. By drawing attention to the impossibility of recuperating the brute material facticity of the body from beneath the proliferation of discourse, however, my intention was never to disavow that body—to suggest, in other words, that it was never "there" in the first place. For me, we can still experience that body negatively as a disturbance within the folds of discourse itself—just as what Lacan calls the hard kernel of the Real can never be encountered directly but only through the moments of rupture in the Symbolic Order. In the ensuing chapters, this gap where the female suffering body should be began to be filled.

For female writers working during the same period as their male counterparts—as we saw in chapter 2—female physical illness and disability are frequently represented through the lens of domesticity. It is striking that the ill female body here is often the body of the (real or potential) mother and the conditions that afflict her concern her ability to perform her maternal role (infertility). However, chapter 2 also observed that, in women's writing of the 1980s and 1990s, the trope of the sick mother undergoes a significant revision. In the later texts, the mother's illness is not merely a lack or inadequacy in her gender role but an essential element in the construction of her own daughter's subjectivity.

Perhaps another way of putting this is to say that, for the younger generation of female writers, female illness and disability become the means toward constructing an inter-generational (auto-) biographical narrative of self-formation. It is again remarkable to note how many of these works contain embedded narratives that stage an implicit generational dialogue between mother and daughter, and more broadly, between a traditional order of womanhood that is dying out and a new one that is in the process of being born. As we saw in chapter 2, Arab women's writing on female illness and disability often becomes a complex work of mourning for a sick mother whose life and experience must simultaneously be preserved, memorialized, and overcome. For Arab women writers, the task is to reconstruct a distinctly feminine line of resistance stretching from mother to daughter that is capable of defying the regime of silence to which women's lives (and particularly ill women's lives) have been subject. In Hafez's words, the female writers in question are "concerned with granting the voiceless female a mature narrative voice that is truly her own" (1995, 170).

In chapter 3, finally, we examined how contemporary Arab writing by Daoud, Khedairi, and Bitar succeeds in writing the female suffering body into existence. It is only necessary to witness the violent critical reaction to Bitar to appreciate that something significant has changed over the last fifty years. After all, the critic Yaseen Rifa'iya professes to find the representation of Maryam in *Imra'a Min Hadha al-'Asr* to be beyond the textual pale: he denounces the portrait of the sick protagonist as deeply unrealistic (2004, 20). To respond to Rifa'iya, though, I would ask what exactly he means by "realism" in this context: is it (as I suspect) little more than a male-dominated literary tradition for whom the acute reality of the female body in pain must remain shrouded in metaphor? If Bitar's representation of Maryam operates on a new aesthetic terrain that breaks with realist conventions, it is because it refuses to submit to the prevailing tradition of what it means to be female and physically ill. For Maudie Bitar, indeed, Maryam "deserves to be saluted" (2004, 138), because she moves beyond "narrow women's discourse" to offer a transparent portrait of passions and pains that are universal and omnipotent (2004, 135). In her groundbreaking representation of ill female subjectivity, Bitar is not succumbing to fantasy or wish fulfillment so much as challenging the patriarchal stranglehold upon the "reality" of the female suffering body. By seeking to explore the female body in pain from within—as it is felt, lived, and experienced—rather than how it is discursively produced from without, Bitar and her contemporaries offer what Silverman calls "an anatomy of female subjectivity" in relation to illness and disability (1988, x).

Repressing Female Illness and Disability

In drawing this book to a close, however, a few lingering questions remain. To start with, *why* has Arabic literature and culture sought to repress the female body in pain? What is it about that body that has led both male and female writers alike to marginalize it? What are the roots of the patriarchal monopolization of female illness and disability that survive even in the work of contemporary critics like Rifa'iya?

Firstly, I have sought to show how a woman's health in Arab culture has traditionally been perceived as a microcosm of the health of her family and other selves rather than her own. Women have been acculturated to prioritize the health of family members above everything and, in particular, to produce and sustain healthy children. During the last 100 years, this health discourse has also become intimately connected to political discourses of nation building in the context of states like Palestine and Egypt. In her book *Gender and the Making of Modern Medicine in Colonial Egypt,* for example, Hibba Abugideiri analyzes Egyptian medical discourses at the turn of the twentieth century. She argues that this discourse imagined and constructed "the 'modern Egyptian woman' as maternal and domestic certainly, but more interestingly as a pillar of health." For Abugideiri, "Egyptian doctors linked women's health and bodily functions with Egypt's societal advancement" (2010, 1).[4] Such a "scientific discourse" aimed to underscore the "maternal and domestic instinct in women for the political purpose of modern nation building" and had a huge impact on women's social behavior and their maternal role more generally (Abugideiri 2010, 1–2). This biopoliticization of maternity is rehearsed in contemporary Palestinian discourses on nationhood, which, as we have seen, repeatedly emphasize reproductive health as a means of saving the Palestinian nation.

To be sure, Arab culture continues even today to valorize the health of women as a signifier of the health of the family, the society, and the nation as a whole. It almost goes without saying by now that the reverse

4. For Abugideiri, this link is apparent in contemporary medical literature. In a 1902 article in a well-known Egyptian medical journal, a doctor advises women on the proper steps to follow to maintain health especially during pregnancy and following delivery. As he urges Egyptian urban women to "exercise more and expose themselves to fresh air," he also encapsulates the very idea that was at the heart of Egyptian medical discourse: " . . . to have a strong body in order to have healthy children" (quoted in Abugideiri 2010, 1).

logic also applies: any symptom of female illness or disability becomes a sign of social or maternal lack and thus undermines a woman's familial and social capital. As a consequence, female illness and disability in Arab culture—particularly in rural areas—remains the subject of social stigmatization. For anthropologist Hind Khattab, sick and ill women are silent (and silenced) subjects who even go so far as to avoid visiting the doctor in order to keep their condition hidden (1992). The inability to live out a gendered role prescribed by society means that the ill/disabled female subject becomes an instance of what Parsons calls "social deviance" (1991, 280–87). This becoming-deviant is an inevitable consequence of a failure to perform "normality" because, as Goffman asserts, "to be a given kind of person . . . is not merely to possess the required attributes, but also to sustain the standards of conduct and appearance that one's social group attaches thereto" (Goffman 1969, 81). In her failure to successfully perform the role she has been assigned, the sick female subject is positioned outside the social norm.

Perhaps another answer to the question of why the female suffering body has been repressed for so long is the historic intimacy between Islamic and health discourses in the Arab world. It is possible to contend that the emphasis on patience and resignation in Islamic theology has, to some degree, wielded passive patients. As we saw in the Introduction, Islamic health discourses in no way discouraged the unwell from seeking treatment, but there is still a risk that pious sick subjects find "social and psychological relief" from the suffering they encounter in God (Sholkamy 2004, 115). For many women, Islam's spiritual quietism mistakenly translated itself into a medical passivity, thus compounding the cultural prohibition on articulating their illness and/or seeking medical help. In this respect, health discourses in Islam have exacerbated the pervading sense that quiet stoicism is the only correct cultural response to female illness and disability.

Writing the Female Suffering Body

Finally, though, one pressing question is left to us. Why has the female suffering body suddenly come into such sharp textual focus in contemporary Arabic literature? What precisely has triggered the focus on the ill female body in a literary tradition that has, for so long, repressed representations of female illness and disability? Perhaps more generally, what social, cultural, and political forces have given rise to this new wave of Arab writing on female, embodiment, illness, and disability?

It is possible to find one, albeit provisional, answer to such questions in the radical social and political changes in the Levant and Egypt over the last fifty years.[5] After all, Hafez has rightly contended that socio-political changes in the Arab world have also been intimately connected to aesthetic changes in the world of Arabic fiction via a complex feedback loop (1994, 93–112). Firstly, then, the turn to the body in recent Arabic literature is an antidote to the collapse of the collective national and political ideology of pan-Arabism. To put it in more historical terms, Arab nationalism's painstaking construction of a monolithic collective subjectivity—an edifice which was already showing cracks by 1960—imploded entirely in the 1970s and 1980s, and what was left behind was the individual, internalized subject of postmodernity.[6] The once "open geographical territory" was taken over by a "closed urban space" as the previous homogenous national self disintegrated across the Arab region. This gave rise to a preoccupation with the individual self and identity, both in society at large and in literary narratives (Hafez 1994, 95). In one sobering sense, then, we might argue that the welcome emergence of the female suffering body in literature and culture is bought at the (considerable) cost of the final disintegration of the pan-Arab dream.

At the same time, the last 50 years have witnessed a number of other social movements which have loosened the patriarchal grip upon the Arab social imaginary: Arab women have become increasingly educated,

5. If my focus here is on a specifically Arab answer to this question, it is possible to find other explanations for the emergence of female physical illness and disability by looking outside the Arab world. It is well documented, for instance, that the last thirty years have witnessed a proliferation of popular discourse upon health, illness, and disability in the West. In this conclusion, however, I am interested in the specifically Arab cultural context.

6. In Hafez's account, this retreat from collectivity into interiority was precipitated by such events as Egypt's defeat in the 1967 War (and the period of intense self-reflection that defeat generated) and Lebanon's descent into Civil War in 1975 (1994, 95).

more active in the public sphere, and more vocal and active in pursuing women's rights. For a new wave of Arab women writers emerging in the late 1950s and 1960s, it became possible to write about women's lives, experiences, and suffering in a new way. To begin with, Arab women writers understandably preferred to stress the social and psychological lives of their female protagonists over their physicality but, as women's writing developed, they became more willing to represent female subjectivity on all levels, including the body. In the same way as their male counterparts, thus, Arab women writers turned inward from the body politic to individual bodies.

For contemporary Arab writers, both male and female alike, then, the body has become the place where some kind of precarious individual subjectivity might be salvaged from the wreckage of the national collective self. It is almost as if the trauma accompanying the loss of a collective identity, which had been anchored in notions of liberation from colonial forces, has been compensated for by a desire to celebrate the freedom of the body from all social, cultural, and sexual restrictions. At the same time, of course, the turn to the body in Arabic literature is by no means uniform and varies in degree and intensity as we move from one political locale to the next. To be sure, it is no coincidence that Arabic literature which emerges out of, or reflects back upon, political violence should be more than usually obsessed with the physical and corporeal legacy of war, occupation, resistance, or sectarian struggle. On the one hand, for example, the Lebanese novel (and in particular such figures as Daoud and al-Daif)[7] bears witness to the singular integrity of a physical body that is constantly under threat of annihilation by political and ideological violence during the Civil War. On the other hand, the Iraqi novel also seeks to ground the social, economic, and political crises of the last twenty years in the fragile but enduring physical body of the individual and the

7. It is worth noting that in al-Daif's forthcoming novel *Hirrat Sikreeda* (Sikreeda's Cat), an exploration of the sexuality of a disabled female character is described in great detail, thus attesting to the ways in which disabled female characters are no longer rendered invisible in both male and female writings.

community. Perhaps most significantly, though, I want to propose that Arabic literature's reflections upon the traumatized body—both natural and political—have finally broken the code of silence that surrounds representations of the female suffering body. In a world where all bodies are suffering, the female suffering body is no longer the exception but the rule, no longer the transgression but the norm.

In conclusion, then, I would argue that it is the turn to the individual body in the wake of external and internal trauma in the body politic that finally enables Arabic literature to write the female body in pain. It is no coincidence, after all, that so many of the female illness narratives we have discussed in this book are at one and the same time narratives of war, destruction, and disease. As we saw in the case of Daoud and Khedairi, for example, the recuperation of the materiality of female illness and disability is enabled by a new sensitivity to the precarious materiality of all life in zones of conflict. To put it most simply, it is out of the debris of the last fifty years of Arab history that the female suffering body of Bitar's Maryam finally emerges. By giving flesh and form to Maryam and her sisters, contemporary Arabic literature has liberated them from the margins to which their earlier equivalent, Mahfouz's Amina, was consigned. Perhaps, though, it is appropriate to end this book by asking what future representations of female illness and disability will look like as we now enter another time of Arab popular revolution, another struggle for self-determination, and, tragically, another descent into counter-revolution, civil war, and sectarian violence. If the argument of this book has been that the collapse of a collective Arab identity has given rise to the privatized, individual body dramatized by contemporary Arabic literature, the inevitable question now arises of what new forms of subjectivity, representation, and identity will emerge out of the complex, dynamic, and ongoing events now unfolding in Tunisia, Bahrain, Egypt, Syria, and other countries. What will be the fate of the female suffering body after the "Arab Spring"?

REFERENCES

◆

INDEX

REFERENCES

English

Abou-Khalil, Jahda. 2005. "Women With Disabilities in Lebanon." *Al-Raida*, Arab Women and Disability, 22(108):13–16.

Abou-Saleh, Mohammed T., Yahia Younis, and Lina Karim. 1998. "Anorexia Nervosa in an Arab Culture." *International Journal of Eating Disorders* 23(2):207–12.

Abugideiri, Hibba. 2010. *Gender and the Making of Modern Medicine in Colonial Egypt*. Farnham, UK: Ashgate.

Abu-Habib, Lina. 1997. *Gender and Disability: Women's Experiences in the Middle East*. London: Oxfam.

Abul-Husn, Randa. 1994. "Women and the HIV/AIDS: A Heterosexual Disease in Lebanon and the Middle East." *Al-Raida*, Women's Health in Lebanon, 11(67):14–16.

Accad, Evelyne. 1984. "The Prostitute in Arab and North African Fiction." In *The Image of the Prostitute in Modern Literature*, edited by Pierre L. Horn and Mary Beth Pringle, 63–75. New York: Frederick Ungar.

———. 1990. *Sexuality and War: Literary Masks of the Middle East*. New York: New York University Press.

———. 1993. "Rebellion, Maturity and the Social Context: Arab Women's Special Contribution to Literature." In *Arab Women: Old Boundaries, New Frontiers*, edited by Judith E. Tucker, 224–53. Bloomington: Indiana University Press.

———. 1994. "My Journey With Cancer." *Al-Raida*, Women's Health in Lebanon 11(67):10–13.

———. 2001. *The Wounded Breast: Intimate Journeys Through Cancer*. North Melbourne, Australia: Spinifex.

Aghacy, Samira. 2000. "To See with the Naked Eye: Problems of Vision in Hassan Daoud's *The Mathilde Building*." *Arabic and Middle Eastern Literatures* 3(2):205–17.

Alexander, Elizabeth. 1994. "Coming Out Blackened and Whole: Fragmentation and Reintegration in Audre Lorde's Zami and the Cancer Journals." *American Literary History* 6(4):695–715.

al-Ali, Nadje. 2000. *Sanctions on Iraq: Background, Consequences, Strategies.* Cambridge: Campaign Against Sanctions on Iraq.

Allen, Roger. 1982. *The Arabic Novel: An Historical and Critical Introduction.* Syracuse: Syracuse University Press.

———. 1995. "The Arabic Short Story and the Status of Women." In *Love and Sexuality in Modern Arabic Literature*, edited by Roger Allen, Hillary Kilpatrick, and Ed de Moor, 77–90. London: Saqi Books.

Atwood, Margaret. 1981. *Bodily Harm.* Toronto: McClelland and Stewart.

Augé, Marc, and Claudine Herzlich, eds. 1995. *The Meaning of Illness: Anthropology, History and Sociology.* Luxembourg: Harwood Academic.

Austen, Jane. 1998. *Persuasion.* London: Penguin Classics.

Badran, Margot. 1995. *Feminists, Islam, and Nation: Gender and the Making of Modern Egypt.* Princeton: Princeton University Press.

Bakare Yusuf, Bibi. 1999. "The Economy of Violence: Black Bodies and the Unspeakable Terror." In *Feminist Theory and the Body: A Reader*, edited by Janet Price and Margrit Shildrick, 311–23. New York: Routledge.

Bakhtin, M. M. 1981. *The Dialogic Imagination: Four Essays.* Translated by Caryl Emerson and Michael Holquist and edited by Michael Holquist. Austin: Texas University Press.

———. 1984. *Problems of Dostoyevski's Poetics.* Translated and edited by Caryl Emerson. Minneapolis: University of Michigan Press.

———. 1990. "Author and Hero in Aesthetic Activity." In *Art and Answerability: Early Philosophical Essays.* Translated by Vadim Liapunov and edited by Michael Holquist and Vadim Liapunov, 4–256. Austin: University of Texas Press.

Bakr, Salwa. 1992. *Wiles of Men and Other Stories.* Translated by D. J. Davies. London: Quartet Books.

———. 1995. *The Golden Chariot.* Translated by Dinah Manisty. Reading, UK: Garnet.

Barker, Clare. 2011. *Postcolonial Fiction and Disability: Exceptional Children, Metaphor and Materiality.* London: Palgrave Macmillan.

Baron, Beth. 2005. *Egypt as a Woman: Nationalism, Gender, and Politics.* Berkeley: University of California Press.

Basyouny, Iman Farid. 1998. *Just a Gaze: Female Clientele of Diet Clinics in Cairo: An Ethnomedical Study.* Cairo: The American University in Cairo Press.

Baym, Nina. 1993. *Women's Fiction: A Guide to Novels by and about Women in America*. 2d ed. Urbana: University of Illinois Press.

Berada, Muhamad. 2014. Review of *Makyaj Khafif li-Hadhih al-Layla* by Hasan Daoud. *al-Hayat*, January 26.

Berger, John. 1972. *Ways of Seeing*. London and Harmondsworth: BBC and Penguin.

Bitar, Maudie. 2004. "Thoroughly Modern Maryam." Review of *Imra'a Min Hadha al-'Asr*, by Haifa' Bitar. Translated by Issa J. Boullata. *Banipal* 21:135–38.

Blaxter, Mildred, and Elizabeth Paterson. 1982. *Mothers and Daughters: A Three Generational Study of Health Attitudes and Behaviour*. London: Heinman Educational Books.

———. 1983. "The Causes of Disease: Women Talking." *Social Science and Medicine* 17(2):59–69.

———. 2004. *Health*. Cambridge, UK: Polity.

Boehmer, Elleke. 2005. *Stories of Women: Gender and Narrative in the Postcolonial Nation*. Manchester and New York: Manchester University Press.

Bollas, Christopher. 1993. *Being a Character: Psychoanalysis and Self-Experience*. London: Routledge.

Booth, Marilyn. 1994. Review of *Fragments of Memory* by Hanna Mina. *World Literature Today* 68(4):877–78.

Brody, Howard. 2003. *Stories of Sickness*. 2d ed. New York: Oxford University Press.

Brooks, Peter. 1993. *Body Work: Objects of Desire in Modern Narrative*. Cambridge, MA: Harvard University Press.

Bury, Michael. 1997. *Health and Illness in a Changing Society*. London: Routledge.

———. 2001. "Illness Narratives: Fact or Fiction?" *Sociology of Health and Illness* 23(3): 263–85.

Butler, Judith. 1993. *Bodies that Matter: On the Discursive Limits of "Sex."* New York: Routledge.

Chedid, Andrée. 2000. *Le Sommeil délivré*. Paris: Editions J'ai lu.

Chodorow, Nancy. 1974. "Family Structures and Feminine Personality." In *Women, Culture and Society*, edited by Michelle Zimbalist Rosaldo and Louise Lamphere, 43–66. Stanford: Stanford University Press.

———. 1978. "Mothering, Object-Relations and the Female Oedipal Configuration." *Feminist Studies* 4(1):137–58.

Cixous, Hélène. 1976. "Viewpoint: The Laugh of the Medusa." Translated by Keith Cohen and Paula Cohen. *Signs* 1(4):875–93.

Clarke, Morgan. 2006. "Islam, Kinship and New Reproductive Technology." *Anthropology Today* 22(5):17–20.

Clouser, Danner K., Charles M. Culver, and Bernard Gert. 1981. "Malady: A New Treatment of Disease." *Hastings Center Report* 11(3):29–37.

Cooke, Miriam. 1987. *War's Other Voices: Women Writers on the Lebanese Civil War.* Cambridge, UK: Cambridge University Press.

———. 1993. "Men Constructed in the Mirror of Prostitution." In *Najuib Mahfouz: From Regional Fame to World Recognition,* edited by Michael Beard and Adnan Haydar, 106–25. Syracuse: Syracuse University Press.

Corker, Mairian, and Tom Shakespeare. 2002. "Mapping the Terrain." In *Disability/ Postmodernity: Embodying Disability Theory,* edited by Mairian Corker and Tom Shakespeare, 1–17. London: Continuum.

Creyghton, Marielouise. 1977. "Communication Between Peasant and Doctor in Tunisia." *Social Science & Medicine* 11:319–24.

Daoud, Hassan. 1999. *The House of Mathilde.* Translated by Peter Theroux. London: Granta.

———. 2009. *Borrowed Time.* Translated by Michael K. Scott. London: Telegram Books.

Davis, Lennard J. 1995. *Enforcing Normalcy: Disability, Deafness and the Body.* London: Verso.

Deheuvels, Luc-Willy, Barbara Michalak-Pikulska, and Paul Starkey, eds. 2006. *Intertexuality in Modern Arabic Literature since 1967.* Durham Modern Language Series. Durham, NC: Durham University Press.

Deshazer, Mary K. 2005. *Fractured Borders: Reading Women's Cancer Literature.* Ann Arbor: University of Michigan Press.

Dinnerstein, Dorothy. 1976. *The Mermaid and the Minotaur: Sexual Arrangements and the Human Malaise.* New York: Harper and Row.

Djebar, Assia. 1993. *Fantasia: An Algerian Cavalcade.* Translated by Dorothy S. Blair. Portsmouth, NH: Heinemann.

———. 2001. *L'Amour, la Fantasia.* Paris: Librairie Générale Française.

Doane, Mary Ann. 1981. "The Woman's Stake: Filming the Female Body." *October* 17:23–36.

Douglas, Ann. 1996. *The Feminization of American Culture.* London: Papermac.

Douglas, Mary. 1996. *Natural Symbols: Explorations in Cosmology.* London and New York: Routledge.

Early, Evelyn A. 1988. "The Baladi Curative System of Cairo, Egypt." *Culture, Medicine and Psychiatry* 12(1):65–83.

———. 1993. "Fertility and Fate: Medical Practices Among Baladi Women of Cairo." In *Everyday Life in the Muslim Middle East,* edited by Donna Lee Bowen and Evelyn A. Early, 102–8. Bloomington and Indianapolis: Indiana University Press.

Eisenberg, Leon. 1977. "Disease and Illness: Distinction Between Professional and Popular Ideas of Sickness." *Culture, Medicine and Psychiatry* 1(1):9–23.

Elsadda, Hoda. 1996. "Women's Writing in Egypt: Reflections on Salwa Bakr." In *Gendering the Middle East: Emerging Perspectives*, edited by Deniz Kandiyoti, 127–44. London and New York: I. B. Tauris.

———. 2006. "Gendered Citizenship: Discourses on Domesticity in the Second Half of the Nineteenth Century." *Hawwa: Journal of Women of the Middle East and the Islamic World* 4(1):1–28.

———. 2007. "Imaging the 'New Man': Gender and Nation in Arab Literary Narratives in the Early Twentieth Century." *JMEWS: Journal of Middle East Women's Studies* 3(2):31–55.

Epstein, Julia. 1995. *Altered Conditions: Disease, Medicine, and Storytelling*. New York: Routledge.

Fahmy, Khaled. 1998. "Women, Medicine and Power in Nineteenth-Century Egypt." In *Remaking Women: Feminism and Modernity in the Middle East*, edited by Lila Abu-Lughod, 35–75. Princeton: Princeton University Press.

Faour, Mohamed. 1989. "Fertility Policy and Family Planning in the Arab Countries." *Studies in Family Planning* 20(5):254–63.

Faqir, Fadia. 1996a. Introduction to *Mothballs*, by Alia Mamdouh, v–ix.

———. 1996b. *Pillars of Salt*. London: Quartet Books.

Fargues, Philippe. 2000. "Protracted National Conflict and Fertility Change: Palestinians and Israelis in the Twentieth Century." *Population and Development Review* 26(3):441–82.

Foucault, Michel. 1971. "The Discourse on Language." *Orders of Discourse* 10:7–30.

———. 1980. "The Eye of Power." In *Power/Knowledge: Selected Interviews and Other Writings, 1972–1977*. Translated by Colin Gordon et al. and edited by Colin Gordon, 146–65. New York and London: Prentice Hall.

———. 1984. *The Foucault Reader*. Edited by Paul Rabinow. New York: Pantheon.

———. 1990. *The History of Sexuality, Volume 1: An Introduction*. Translated by Robert Hurley. New York: Vintage.

———. 1991. *Discipline and Punish: The Birth of the Prison*. 4th ed. Translated by Alan Sheridan. London and New York: Penguin.

———. 1993. *The Birth of the Clinic: An Archaeology of Medical Perception*. Translated by A. M. Sheridan Smith. New York: Vintage.

Frank, Arthur. 1995. *The Wounded Storyteller: Body, Illness, and Ethics.* Chicago: University of Chicago Press.

———. 1997. "Illness as Moral Occasion: Restoring Agency to Ill People." *Health* 1(2):131–48.

Freidson, Eliot. 1970. "The Social Construction of Illness." In *Profession of Medicine: A Study of the Sociology of Applied Knowledge,* 203–302. New York: Harper and Row.

Freud, Sigmund. 1963. *Three Case Histories.* New York: Macmillan.

Furst, Lilian A. 2003. *Idioms of Distress: Psychosomatic Disorders in Medical and Imaginative Literature.* Albany: State University of New York Press.

Gallagher, Jean. 1998. *The World Wars through the Female Gaze.* Carbondale: Southern Illinois University Press.

Gardiner, Judith Kegan. 1978. "A Wake for the Mother: The Maternal Deathbed in Women's Fiction." *Feminist Studies* 4(2):146–65.

Garfield, Richard, and Beth Osborne Daponte. 2000. "The Effect of Economic Sanctions on the Mortality of Iraqi Children Prior to the 1991 Persian Gulf War." *American Journal of Public Health* 90(4):546–52.

Gilbert, Sandra, and Susan Gubar. 1979. *The Madwoman in the Attic: The Woman Writer and the Nineteenth-Century Literary Imagination.* New Haven: Yale University Press.

Gilman, Charlotte Perkins. 1981. *The Yellow Wallpaper and Other Stories.* New York: Virago Press.

Gilman, Sander L. 1988. *Disease and Representation: Images of Illness from Madness to Aids.* Ithaca: Cornell University Press.

Gitter, Elizabeth G. 1999. "The Blind Daughter in Charles Dickens's *Cricket on the Hearth.*" *Studies in English Literature, 1500–1900,* The Nineteenth Century 39(4):675–89.

Goffman, Erving. 1963. *Behaviour in Public Places: Notes on the Social Organization of Gatherings.* London: The Free Press of Glencoe, Collier-Mcmillan Ltd.

———. 1969. *The Presentation of Self in Everyday Performance.* London: Allen Lane.

———. 1974. *Frame Analysis: An Essay on the Organization of Experience.* New York: Harper and Row.

———. 1976. *Gender Advertisements.* London: Macmillan.

———. 1990. *Stigma: Notes on the Management of Spoiled Identity.* London: Penguin.

Good, Byron J. 1994. *Medicine, Rationality, and Experience: An Anthropological Perspective.* Cambridge, UK: Cambridge University Press.

Good, Mary-Jo DelVechio et al., eds. 1992. *Pain as Human Experience: An Anthropological Perspective*. Berkeley and London: University of California Press.

Grosz, Elisabeth. 1994. *Volatile Bodies: Toward a Corporeal Feminism*. Bloomington: Indiana University Press.

Hafez, Sabry. 1984. "The Maturation of a Literary Genre." *International Journal of Middle East Studies* 16(3):367–89.

———. 1994. "The Transformation of Reality and the Arabic Novel's Aesthetic Response." *Bulletin of the School of Oriental and African Studies* 57(1):93–112.

———. 1995. "Women's Narrative in Modern Arabic Literature: A Typology." In *Love and Sexuality in Modern Arabic Literature*, edited by Roger Allen, Hilary Kilpatrick, and Ed de Moor, 154–74. London: Saqi Books.

———. 2001. Introduction to *The Cairo Trilogy*, by Naguib Mahfouz, vii–xxiii. New York and London: Knopf.

el-Hamamsy, Laila. 1972. "Belief Systems and Family Planning in Peasant Societies." In *Are Our Descendants Doomed?*, edited by Harrison Brownn and Edward Hutchings, 335–57. New York: Viking.

Hardey, Michael. 1998. *The Social Context of Health*. Buckingham and Philadelphia, PA: Open University Press.

Harlow, Barbara. 1992. "Introduction: 'In *The Golden Chariot* Things Will Be Better.'" *boundary 2*, Feminism and Postmodernism 19(2):150–62.

———. 1996. "History and Endings: Ghassan Kanafani and the Politics of Terminations in Palestine." In *After Lives: Legacies of Revolutionary Writing*, 43–75. London: Verso.

Hatem, Mervat F. 1997. "The Professionalization of Health and the Control of Women's Bodies as Modern Governmentalities in Nineteenth-Century Egypt." In *Women in the Ottoman Empire: Middle East Women in the Early Modern Era*, edited by Madeleine C. Zilfi, 66–80. Leiden: Brill.

Herndl, Diane Price. 1993. *Invalid Women: Figuring Feminine Illness in American Fiction and Culture 1840–1940*. Chapel Hill: The University of North Carolina Press.

Herzlich, Claudine. 1973. *Health and Illness: A Social Psychological Analysis*. London: Academic Press.

Herzlich, Claudine, and Janine Pierret. 1985. "The Social Construction of the Patient: Patients and Illnesses in Other Ages." *Social Science and Medicine* 20(2):145–51.

———. 1987. *Illness and Self in Society*. Translated by Elborg Forster. Baltimore and London: The Johns Hopkins University Press.

Hirsch, Marianne. 1989. *The Mother/Daughter Plot: Narrative, Psychoanalysis, Feminism*. Bloomington: Indiana University Press.

Hite, Molly. 1989. *The Other Side of the Story: Structures and Strategies of Contemporary Feminist Narratives*. New York: Cornell University Press.

Howson, Alexandra. 2004. *The Body in Society: An Introduction*. Cambridge, UK: Polity.

Hyden, Lars-Christer. 1997. "Illness and Narrative." *Sociology of Health and Illness* 19(1):48–69.

Ingstad, Benedcite, and Susan Reynolds Whyte, eds. 1995. "Disability and Culture: An Overview." In *Disability and Culture*, 3–32. Berkeley and London: University of California Press.

Inhorn, Marcia C. 1994. *Quest for Conception: Gender, Infertility, and Egyptian Medical Traditions*. Philadelphia: University of Pennsylvania Press.

———. 2003. *Local Babies, Global Science: Gender, Religion, and In Vitro Fertilization in Egypt*. New York: Routledge.

———. 2006. "Defining Women's Health: A Dozen Messages from More than 150 Ethnographies." *Medical Anthropology Quarterly* 20(3):345–78.

———. 2012. *The New Arab Man: Emergent Masculinities, Technologies, and Islam in the Middle East*. Princeton: Princeton University Press.

Irigaray, Luce. 1985. *This Sex Which is Not One*. Translated by Catherine Porter. Ithaca: Cornell University Press.

James, Henry. 2008. *The Wings of the Dove*. London and New York: Penguin Classics.

Kabbara, Nawaf. 2005a. "On Disabilities." *Al-Raida*, Arab Women and Disability 22(108):2.

———. 2005b. "Women with Disability: The Peculiarity of the Case." *Al-Raida*, Arab Women and Disability 22(18):10–12.

Kamal, Montasser M. 2004. "Fi nas wi fi nas: Class Culture and Illness Practice in Egypt." In *Health and Identity in Egypt*, edited by Hania Sholkamy and Farha Ghannam, 65–90.

Kammer, Jeanne. 1979. "The Art of Silence and the Forms of Women's Poetry." In *Shakespeare's Sisters: Feminist Essays on Women Poets*, edited by Sandra Gilbert and Susan Gubar, 153–82. Bloomington: Indiana University Press.

Kanaaneh, Rhoda Ann. 2002. *Birthing the Nation: Strategies of Palestinian Women in Israel*. Berkeley and Los Angeles: University of California Press.

Kanafani, Ghassan. 1978. *Men in the Sun and Other Palestinian Stories*. Translated by Hilary Kilpatrick, 9–56. London: Heinmann; Washington, D.C.: Three Continents Press.

Kaplan, Ann E. 1992. *Motherhood and Representation: The Mother in Popular Culture and Melodrama*. London and New York: Routledge.

Kehinde, Ayo. 2003. "The Contemporary Arabic Novel as Social History: Urban Decadence, Politics and Women in Naguib Mahfouz's Fiction." *Studies in the Humanities* 30(1–2):144–63.

Kelly, Michael P., and David Field. 1996. "Medical Sociology, Chronic Illness and the Body." *Sociology of Health and Illness* 18(2):241–57.

Khattab, Hind. 1992. *The Silent Endurance: Social Conditions of Women's Reproductive Health in Rural Egypt*. Amman: Population Council/UNICEF.

Khattab, Hind, Nabil Younis, and Huda Zurak. 2000. *Women, Reproduction, and Health in Rural Egypt: The Giza Study*. Cairo: The American University in Cairo Press.

Khedairi, Betool. 2001. *A Sky So Close*. Translated by Muhayman Jamil. New York: Pantheon Books.

———. 2005. *Absent*. Translated by Muhayman Jamil. Cairo: The American University in Cairo Press.

el-Kholy, Heba. 2004. "A Discourse of Resistance: Spirit Possession among Women in Low-Income Cairo." In *Health and Identity in Egypt*, edited by Hania Sholkamy and Farha Ghannam, 21–41. Cairo and New York: The American University in Cairo Press.

Khoury, Colette. 1957. *Vingt Ans*. Beirut: n.d.

Kilpatrick, Hilary. 1974. *The Modern Egyptian Novel: A Study in Social Criticism*. London: Ithaca Press.

Kleinman, Arthur. 1980. *Patients and Healers in the Context of Culture: An Exploration of the Borderland Between Anthropology, Medicine, and Psychiatry*. Berkeley and London: University of California Press.

———. 1988. *The Illness Narratives: Suffering, Healing, and the Human Condition*. New York: Basic Books.

Kleinman, Arthur, and Joan Kleinman. 1994. "How Bodies Remember: Social Memory and Bodily Experience of Criticism, Resistance, and Delegitimation Following China's Cultural Revolution." *New Literary History* 25(3):707–23.

Kleinman, Arthur, Leon Eisenberg, and Byron Good. 1978. "Culture, Illness and Care: Clinical Lessons From Anthropologic and Cross-Cultural Research." *Annals of Internal Medicine* 88(2):251–58.

———. 2006. "Culture, Illness and Care: Clinical Lessons from Anthropologic and Cross-Cultural Research." *FOCUS: The Journal of Lifelong Learning in Psychiatry* 4(1):140–49.

Kuhnke, LaVerne. 1974. "The Doctoress on a Donkey: Women Health Officers in Nineteenth-Century Egypt." *Clio Medica* 9(3):193–205.

Lacan, Jacques. 1977. *The Four Fundamental Concepts of Psychoanalysis.* Translated by Alan Sheridan. New York: W. W. Norton and Co.

———. 2004. "The Mirror Stage as Formative of the Function of the I as Revealed in Psychoanalytic Experience." In *Ecrits,* selected and translated by Alan Sheridan, 1–8. London and New York: Routledge Classics.

Lane, Sandra D., and Robert A. Rubinstein. 1991. "The Use of Fatwas in the Production of Reproductive Health Policy in Egypt." Paper presented at the Ninetieth Annual Meeting of the American Anthropological Association, Chicago.

Latour, Bruno. 1993. *We Have Never Been Modern.* Translated by Catherine Porter. Cambridge, MA: Harvard University Press.

Laurence, Patricia Ondek. 1991. *The Reading of Silence: Virginia Woolf in the English Tradition.* Stanford: Stanford University Press.

Layoun, Mary N. 1990. "Deserts of Memory." In *Travels of a Genre: The Modern Novel and Ideology,* 177–208. Princeton: Princeton University Press.

Le Gassick, Trevor. 1991. "Introduction." In *Critical Perspectives on Naguib Mahfouz,* edited by Trevor Le Gassick, 1–8. Washington, D.C.: Three Continents Press.

Lewis, Aubrey. 1953. "Health as Social Concept." *The British Journal of Sociology* 4(2):109–24.

Lorde, Audre. 1980a. "After Breast Cancer: I am a Warrior, Not a Victim." *Savvy* (April):68–69.

———. 1980b. *The Cancer Journals.* London: Sheba Feminist Publishers.

———. 1982. *Zami: A New Spelling of My Name.* London: Sheba Feminist Publishers.

———. 1988. *A Burst of Light.* New York: Firebrand Books.

Lupton, Deborah. 1994. *Medicine as Culture: Illness, Disease and the Body in Western Societies.* London and Thousand Oaks, CA: Sage.

Mahfouz, Naguib. 1990. *Palace Walk: The Cairo Trilogy 1.* Translated by William Maynard Hutchins and Olive E. Kenny. Doubleday: London and New York.

———. 1991. *Palace of Desire: The Cairo Trilogy 11.* Translated by William Maynard Hutchins, Lorne M. Kenny, and Olive E. Kenny. Doubleday: London and New York.

———. 1992. *Sugar Street: The Cairo Trilogy 111.* Translated by William Maynard Hutchins and Angele Botros Semaan. Doubleday: London and New York.

Mahmoud, Fatma Moussa. 1973. *The Arabic Novel in Egypt: 1940–1970.* Cairo: General Egyptian Book Organization.

Malin, Jo. 2000. *The Voice of the Mother: Embedded Maternal Narratives in Twentieth-Century Autobiographies.* Carbondale and Edwardsville: Southern Illinois University Press.

Malti-Douglas, Fedwa. 1988. *Blindness and Autobiography: Al-Ayyam of Taha Husayn.* Princeton: Princeton University Press.

———. 1991. *Woman's Body, Woman's Word: Gender and Discourse in Arabo-Islamic Writing.* Princeton: Princeton University Press.

———. 1995. "Social Power, Body Power." In *Men, Women, and God(s): Nawal El Saadawi and Arab Feminist Poetics,* 20–43. Berkeley: University of California Press.

———. 2001. *Medicines of the Soul: Female Bodies and Sacred Geographies in a Transnational Islam.* Berkeley: University of California Press.

Mamdouh, Alia. 1996. *Mothballs.* Translated by Peter Theroux. Reading, UK: Garnet.

Manisty, Dinah. 1994. "Madness as Textual Strategy in the Narratives of Three Egyptian Women Writers." *Alif: Journal of Comparative Poetics,* Madness and Civilization (14):152–74.

Marshal, Helen. 1999. "Our Bodies, Ourselves: Why We Should Add Old Fashioned Empirical Phenomenology to the New Theories of the Body." In *Feminist Theory and the Body: A Reader,* 64–75. New York: Routledge.

Masri, Rania. 2003. "Assault on Iraq's Environment: The Continuing Effects of Depleted Uranium Weaponry and Blockade." In *Iraq: Its History, People and Politics,* edited by Shams C. Inati, 189–213. New York: Humanity Books.

Mernissi, Fatima. 1977. "Women, Saints, and Sanctuaries." *Signs* 3(1):101–12.

Meyers, Diana Tietjens. 2001. "The Rush to Motherhood: Pronatalist Discourse and Women's Autonomy." *Signs* 26(3):735–73.

Meyers, Jeffrey. 1985. *Disease and the Novel, 1880–1960.* London: Macmillan.

Michie, Helena. 1987. *The Flesh Made Word: Female Figures and Women's Bodies.* New York and Oxford: Oxford University Press.

———. 1989. "Who is this Pain?": Scarring, Disfigurement, and Female Identity in *Bleak House* and *Our Mutual Friend.*" *NOVEL: A Forum on Fiction* 22(2):199–212.

Mina, Hanna. 1993. *Fragments of Memory.* Translated by Olive Kenny and Lorne Kenny. Austin: University of Texas at Austin, Center for Middle Eastern Studies.

Mitchell, David T. 2002. "Narrative Prosthesis and the Materiality of Metaphor." In *Disability Studies: Enabling the Humanities,* edited by Sharon L. Snyder, Brenda Jo Brueggemann, and Rosemarie Garland-Thompson, 15–30. New York: Modern Language Association of America.

Mitchell, David. T., and Sharon L. Snyder. 2000. *Narrative Prosthesis: Disability and the Dependencies of Discourse.* Ann Arbor: University of Michigan Press.

———. 2004. "Introduction: Disability Studies and the Double Bind of Representation." In *The Body and Physical Difference: Discourses of Disability*, edited by David T. Mitchell and Sharon L. Snyder. Ann Arbor: University of Michigan Press.

Morris, Jenny, ed. 1996. *Encounters with Strangers: Feminism and Disability.* London: Women's Press.

Morsy, Soheir. 1978. "Sex Roles, Power and Illness in an Egyptian Village." *American Ethnologist: Journal of the American Ethnological Society* 5(1):137–50.

———. 1993. *Gender, Sickness and Healing in Egypt: Ethnography in Historical Context.* Boulder, CO: Westview Press.

Mulvey, Laura. 1977. "Visual Pleasure and Narrative Cinema." In *Women and the Cinema: A Critical Anthology*, edited by Karen Kay and Gerald Peary, 412–28. New York: Dutton.

Murphy, Robert F. 1990. *The Body Silent.* New York and London: W. W. Norton.

Nead, Lynda. 2007. *The Female Nude: Art, Obscenity and Sexuality.* 3d ed. London and New York: Routledge.

Nelson, Cynthia. 1971. "Self, Spirit Possession and World View: An Illustration from Egypt." *International Journal of Social Psychiatry* 17(3):194–209.

———. 1977. "Notes on the Development of a First Course in Social Sciences of Health and Healing in the Arab Republic of Egypt." *Medical Anthropological Newsletter* 9(1):19–22.

O'Connor, Flannery. 1955. *A Good Man is Hard to Find and Other Stories.* New York: Harcourt, Brace and Company.

———. 1965. *Everything that Rises Must Converge.* New York: Farrar, Straus and Giroux.

Ostle, Robin, ed. 1991. *Modern Literature in the Near and Middle East.* London and New York: Routledge.

———. 1995. "The Romantic Imagination and the Female Ideal." In *Love and Sexuality in Modern Arabic Literature*, 33–45.

Papashvily, Helen W. 1956. *All the Happy Endings: A Study of the Domestic Novel in America, the Women Who Wrote It, the Women Who Read It in the Nineteenth Century.* New York: Harper and Brothers.

Parsons, Talcott. 1991. *The Social System.* New ed. London: Routledge.

Pollard, Lisa. 2005. *Nurturing the Nation: The Family Politics of Modernizing, Colonizing and Liberating Egypt, 1805–1923.* Berkeley and Los Angeles: University of California Press.

Poovey, Mary. 1988. *Uneven Developments: The Ideological Work of Gender in Mid-Victorian England*. Chicago: University of Chicago Press.

———. 1990. "Speaking of the Body: Mid-Victorian Constructions of Female Desire." In *Body/Politics: Women and Discourse of Science*, edited by Mary Jacobus, Evelyn Fox Keller, and Sally Shuttleworth, 29–46. New York and London: Routledge.

Punday, Daniel. 2003. *Narrative Bodies: Toward a Corporeal Narratology*. New York: Palgrave Macmillan.

Radley, Alan. 1993. "Introduction." In *Worlds of Illness: Biographical and Cultural Perspectives on Health and Disease*, edited by Alan Radley, 1–8. London: Routledge.

Rajchman, John. 1988. "Foucault's Art of Seeing." *October* 44:88–117.

Ramsay, Gail. 1996. *The Novels of an Egyptian Romanticist: Yusuf al-Siba'i*. Edsbruk: Akademitryck AB.

Rich, Adrienne. 1976. *Of Women Born: Motherhood as Experience and Institution*. New York: W. W. Norton and Co.

———. 1978. *The Dream of a Common Language: Poems 1974–1977*. New York: W. W. Norton and Co.

al-Saadawi, Nawal. 1989. *Memoirs of a Woman Doctor*. Translated by Catherine Cobham. San Francisco: City Lights.

Salameh, Fahd A. A. 2000. *The Jordanian Novel 1980–1990: A Study and Assessment*. Amman: Ministry of Culture.

Salem, Elise. 2003. *Constructing Lebanon: A Century of Literary Narratives*. Gainesville: University Press of Florida.

Saliba, Therese. 1996. "On the Bodies of Third World Women: Cultural Impurity, Prostitution, and Other Nervous Conditions." *College Literature* 22(1):131–46.

al-Samaan, Ghada. 1968. "Street Walker." In *Arabic Writing Today: The Short Story*, edited by Mahmoud Manzalaoui, 317–27. Cairo: American Research Center in Egypt.

Sandelowski, Margarete J. 1990. "Failures of Volition: Female Agency and Infertility in Historical Perspective." *Signs* 15(3):475–99.

Scarry, Elaine. 1985. *The Body in Pain*. New York and Oxford: Oxford University Press.

Scheft, Thomas J. 2000. "Shame and the Social Bond: A Sociological Theory." *Sociological Theory* 18(1):84–99.

Schepher-Hughes, Nancy, and Margaret M. Lock. 1986. "Speaking 'Truth' to Illness: Metaphors, Reification, and a Pedagogy for Patients." *Medical Anthropology Quarterly* 17(5):137–40.

Seedhouse, David. 1986. *Health: The Foundations for Achievement*. Chichester: John Wiley.

Seigneurie, Ken. 2008. "Anointing With Rubble: Ruins in the Lebanese War Novel." *Comparative Studies of South Asia, Africa and the Middle East* 28(1):50–60.

———. 2011. *Standing by the Ruins: Elegiac Humanism in Wartime and Postwar Lebanon*. New York: Fordham University Press.

Sexuality and Arab Women. 2002/2003. *Al-Raida* 20(99).

Sheridan, Alan. 1980. *Michel Foucault: The Will to Truth*. New York: Tavistock.

Shildrick, Margrit, and Janet Price. 1999. "Bodies in Science and Biomedicine: An Introduction." In *Feminist Theory and the Body: A Reader*, edited by Price and Shildrick, 145–48.

———. 1999. "Breaking the Boundaries of the Broken Body." In *Feminist Theory and the Body: A Reader*, 432–44.

———. 2002. "Bodies Together: Touch, Ethics and Disability." In *Disability/Postmodernity: Embodying Disability Theory*, edited by Mairian Corker and Tom Shakespeare, 62–75. London and New York: Continuum.

Shilling, Chris. 2003. *The Body and Social Theory*. 2d ed. London; Thousand Oaks, CA; New Delhi: Sage.

Sholkamy, Hania. 2004. "Conclusion: The Medical Cultures of Egypt." In *Health and Identity in Egypt*, 111–28.

Showalter, Elaine, ed. 1985. *New Feminist Criticism: Essays On Women, Literature, and Theory*. New York: Pantheon.

———. 1987. *The Female Malady: Women, Madness and English Culture, 1830–1980*. New York: Penguin.

Siddiq, Muhammad. 1984. *Man is a Cause: Political Consciousness and the Fiction of Ghassan Kanafani*. Seattle and London: University of Washington Press.

Silverman, Kaja. 1988. *The Acoustic Mirror: The Female Voice in Psychoanalysis and Cinema*. Bloomington and Indianapolis: Indiana University Press.

Sontag, Susan. 1990. *Illness as Metaphor and AIDS and Its Metaphor*. New York and London: Anchor Books, Doubleday.

Stacey, Jackie. 1997. *Teratologies: A Cultural Study of Cancer*. London: Routledge.

Starkey, Paul. 2003. "Crisis and Memory in Rachid al-Daif's *Dear Mr. Kawabata*." In *Crisis and Memory: The Representation of Space in Modern Levantine Narrative*, edited by Ken Seigneurie, 115–30. Wiesbaden: Reichert-Verlag.

Suleiman, Susan Rubin. 1985. "Writing and Motherhood." In *The M(o)ther Tongue: Essays in Feminist Psychoanalytical Interpretation*, edited by Shirley Nelson

Garner, Claire Kahane, and Madelon Sprengnether, 352–77. Ithaca: Cornell University Press.

al-Tahawy, Miral. 1998. *The Tent*. Translated by Anthony Calderbank. Cairo: The American University in Cairo Press.

Tapper, Nancy. 1990. "*Ziyarat*: Gender, Movement, and Exchange in a Turkish Community." In *Muslim Travellers: Pilgrimage, Migration, and the Religious Imagination*, edited by Dale F. Eickelman and James Piscatori, 236–55. Berkeley: University of California Press.

Tawilah, Jihane. 1994. "The Lebanon Report for the Regional Workshop on the Role of Women in AIDS Prevention and Control." NACP, Cairo. May 16–18.

Thompson, Elizabeth. 2000. *Colonial Citizens: Republican Rights, Paternal Privilege, and Gender in French Syria and Lebanon*. New York: Columbia University Press.

Turner, Bryan S. 1992. *Regulating Bodies: Essays in Medical Sociology*. London and New York: Routledge.

———. 1996. *The Body and Society: Explorations in Social Theory*. 2d ed. London: Sage.

Turner, Bryan S., and Colin Samson. 1995. *Medical Power and Social Knowledge*. 2d ed. London: Sage.

Ussher, Jane M. 2000. "Women's Health: Contemporary Concerns." In *Women's Health: Contemporary International Perspectives*, edited by Jane M. Ussher, 1–25. Leicester: The British Psychological Society.

Valassopoulos, Anastasia. 2007. *Contemporary Arab Women Writers: Cultural Expression in Context*. London and New York: Routledge.

Wendell, Susan. 1999. "Feminism, Disability and the Transcendence of the Body." In *Feminist Theory and the Body: A Reader*, edited by Price and Shildrick, 324–33.

Wilkinson, Sue, and Celia Kitzinger. 1994. "Towards a Feminist Approach to Breast Cancer." In *Women and Health: Feminist Perspectives*, edited by Sue Wilkinson and Celia Kitzinger, 124–40. Southport, UK: Taylor and Francis.

Williams, Gareth H. 1991. "Disablement and the Ideological Crisis in Health Care." *Social Science and Medicine* 32(4):517–24.

———. 1993. "Chronic Illness and the Pursuit of Virtue in Everyday Life." In *Worlds of Illness: Biographical and Cultural Perspectives on Health and Disease*, edited by Alan Radley, 92–108.

Winterson, Jeanette. 1993. *Written on the Body*. New York: Knopf.

Wood, Ann Douglas. 1973. "'The Fashionable Disease': Women's Complaints and their Treatment in Nineteenth-Century America." *Journal of Interdisciplinary History*, The Historian and the Arts 4(1):25–52.

World Health Organization. 1980. *International Classification of Impairments, Disabilities, and Handicaps*. Geneva: WHO. Reprinted annually.

———. 1990. *Environment and Health: The European Charter and Commentary. WHO Regional Publications Series 35*. Copenhagen: WHO.

———. 2013. "Disability and Health: Fact sheet no. 352." Accessed September 20. http://www.who.int/mediacentre/factsheets/fs352/en/.

Zeidan, Joseph. 1995. *Arab Women Novelists: The Formative Years and Beyond*. Albany: State University of New York Press.

Zeilani, Ruqayya, and Seymour, Jane E. 2010. "Muslim Women's Experiences of Suffering in Jordanian Intensive Care Study Units: A Narrative." *Intensive and Critical Care Nursing* 26(3):175–84.

Zola, Irving Kenneth. 1973. "Pathways to the Doctor—From Person to Patient." *Social Science and Medicine* 7:677–89.

———. 1983. *Socio-Medical Inquiries: Reflections and Reconsiderations*. Philadelphia, PA: Temple University Press.

Zuhur, Sherifa. 1992. "Of Milk-Mothers and Sacred Bonds: Islam, Patriarchy, and New Reproductive Technologies." *Creighton Law Review* 25:1725–38.

Arabic

Abou-Khalil, Jahda. 2001. *Nisa' Takhatayna al-Hawajiz: Wahid wa 'Ishrin Sira Dhatiya li Nisa' Tahadayna al'-'Aka*. Beirut: al-Jam'iya al-Wataniya li-Huquq al-Mu'aq fi Lubnan.

Allah Ma'ana. 1955. Directed by Ahmad Badrakhan.

Ba'albakki, Layla. 1958. *Ana Ahya*. 1st ed. n.d.

———. 1963. *Ana Ahya*. 2d ed. Beirut: Dar Majallat Shi'r.

Bakr, Salwa. 1986. *Zinat fi Janazat al-Ra'is*. Cairo: n.d.

———. 1986. *Maqam 'Atiya*. Cairo: Dar al-Fikr li-al-Dirasat wa-al-Nashr.

———. 1991. *al-'Araba al-Dhahabiya la Tas'ad ila al-Sama'*. Cairo: Sina li-al-Nashr.

———. 1992. *'Ajin al-Fallaha*. Cairo: Sina li-al-Nashr.

———. 1993. *Wasf al-Bulbul*. Cairo: Sina li-al-Nashr.

———. 1997. *Layl wa Nahar*. Cairo: Dar al-Hilal.

———. 2003. *Sawaqi al-Waqt*. Cairo: Dar al-Hilal.

———. 2003. *Shu'ur al-Aslaf*. Cairo: Maktabat Madbuli.

———. 2004. *Kuku Sudan Kibashi*. Cairo: Dar Mirit.

Berada, Muhammad. n.d. Review of *Makyaj Khafif li-Hadhih al-Layla*. *Adab wa Fan*. Accessed August 2009. http://www.adabwafan.com/display/review.asp?.

Bitar, Haifa'. 1994a. *Ghurub wa-Kitaba*. Beirut: Dar an-Nahar.

———. 1994b. *Yawmiyat Mutallaqa*. Damascus: Dar al-Ahali.

———. 1996. *Afrah Saghira, Afrah Kabira*. Damascus: Dar al-Ahali.

———. 1998. *Mawt al-Baj'a*. Damascus: Ittihad al-Kuttab al-'Arab.

———. 1999. *Imra'a min Tabiqayn*. Ladhikiya: Dar Palmira.

———. 2000. *al-Saqita*. Beirut: Dar Riad el-Rayyes.

———. 2004. *Imra'a Min Hadha al-'Asr*. Beirut: Dar al-Saqi.

al-Daif, Rachid. Forthcoming. *Hirrat Sikreeda*. Beirut: al-Saqi.

Daoud, Hasan. 1983. *Binayat Matild*. Beirut: Dar al-Tanwir.

———. 1984. *Tahta Shurfat Anji*. Beirut: Dar al-Tanwir.

———. 1985. *Rawd al-Hayat al-Mahzun*. Beirut: Dar al-Tanwir.

———. 1990. *Ayyam Za'ida*. Beirut: Dar al-Jadid.

———. 1992. *Nuzhat al-Malak*. Beirut: Dar al-Jadid.

———. 1996. *Sanat al-Ottomatic*. Beirut: Dar an-Nahar.

———. 1998. *Ghina' al-Batriq*. Beirut: Dar an-Nahar.

———. 2003. *Makyaj Khafif li-Hadhih al-Layla*. Beirut: Riad el-Rayyes.

Ghanim, Fathi. 1962. *al-Rajul Alladhi Faqada Zillah*. n.d.

———. 1966. *Tilka al-Ayyam*. Cairo: Dar Roz al-Yusuf.

———. 1977. *Zaynab wa-al-'Arsh*. Cairo: Dar Roz al-Yusuf.

al-Hakim, Tawfiq. 1932. *'Awdat al-Ruh*. 2 vols. Cairo: Maktabat al-Adab.

Haqqi, Yahya. 1944. *Qindil Umm Hashim*. Cairo: n.p.

Haydar, Haydar. 1979. *Walima li-a'Shab al-Bahr*. Beirut: Mu'assasat al-Abhath.

Haykal, Muhammad Husayn. 1913. *Zaynab*. n.p., n.d.

Hussayn, Taha. *al-Ayyam*. Cairo: n.p., 1929.

Idris, Yusuf. 1953. "'Ala Asyut." *al-Misri*, March 21.

———. 1965. *Lughat al-Ay Ay*. Cairo: Dar Roz al-Yusuf.

———. 1971. "Ahmad al-Majlis al-Baladi." In *al-Mu'allafat al-Kamilla*, 432–43. Cairo: 'Alam al-Kutub.

Kanafani, Ghassan. 1962. *Rijal fi al-Shams*. Beirut: Dar al-Tali'a.

———. 1964. *al-Bab*. Beirut: Dar al-Tali'a.

———. 1966. *Ma Tabaqqa Lakum*. Beirut: Dar al-Tali'a.

———. 1968. *'An al-Rijal wa-al-Banadiq: Qisas*. Beirut: Dar al-'Awda.

———. 1970. *'A'id ila Hayfa*. Beirut: Dar al-'Awda.

Khedairi, Betool. 1999. *Kam Badat al-Samao' Qariba*. Beirut: al-Mu'assasa al-'Arabiyya li-al-Dirasat wa-al-Nashr, 1999; Aman: Dar al-Faris, 1999.

———. 2004. *Ghayib*. Beirut: al-Mu'assasa al-'Arabiyya li-al-Dirasat wa-al-Nashr.

Khoury, Colette. 1959. *Ayyam Ma'ahu*. n.d.

———. 1961. *Layla Wahida*. Beirut: al-Maktab al-Tijari li-al-Tiba' wa-al-Nashr.

———. 1962. *Ana wa-al-Mada*. Beirut: al-Maktab al-Tijari li-al-Tiba'a wa-al-Nashr.
———. 1968. *Kiyan*: "*Ustura*." n.p.: Manshurat Zuhayr Ba'albakki.
———. 1970. Reprint. *Laylah Wahida*. n.p.: Manshurat Zuhayr Ba'albakki.
———. 1971. *al-Kalima Untha*. Beirut: Manshurat Zuhayr Ba'albakki.
———. 1975. *Wa-Marra Sayf*. Damascus: Ittihad al-Kuttab al-'Arab.
———. 1984. *al-Ayyam al-Mudi'a*. Damascus: Dar Talas.
Khoury, Elias. 1984. *al-Jabal al-Saghir*. Beirut: Mu'assasat al-Abhath al-'Arabiyya.
Mahfouz, Naguib. 1945. *al-Qahira al-Jadida*. n.p.
———. 1947. *Zuqaq al-Midaq*. n.p.
———. 1956. *Bayn al-Qasrayn*. Cairo: Maktabat Misr.
———. 1957a. *Qasr al-Shawq*. Cairo: Maktabat Misr.
———. 1957b. *al-Sukkariya*. Cairo: Maktabat Misr.
———. 1963. "Za'abalawi." In *Dunya Allah*, 135–50. Cairo: Maktabat Misr.
———. 1965. *al-Shahhadh*. Cairo: Maktabat Misr.
———. 1967a. *Awlad Haratina*. Beirut: Dar al-Adab.
———. 1967b. *Miramar*. Cairo: Maktabat Misr.
———. 1973. *al-Hubb Tahta al-Matar*. Cairo: Maktabat Misr.
———. 1975. *Hadrat al-Muhtaram*. Cairo: Maktabat Misr.
———. 1980. *Afrah al-Qubba*. Cairo: Maktabat Misr.
———. 1982. *Baqi min al-Zaman Sa'a*. Cairo: Maktabat Misr.
Mahmoud, Ibrahim. 2002. *al-Shabaq al-Muharram: Antolojya al-Nusus al-Mamnu'a*. Beirut: Riad el-Rayyes.
Mamdouh, Alia. 1973. *Iftitahiya li-al-Dahik*. Beirut: Dar al-'Awda.
———. 1977. *Hawamish ila al-Sayyida 'B'*. Beirut: Dar al-Adab.
———. 1980. *Layla wa-al-Dh'ib*. Baghdad: Dar al-Hurriyya.
———. 1986. *Habbat al-Naftaleen*. Cairo: al-Haya al-Misriyya al-'Ammah li-al-Kitab.
———. 1995. *al-Wala'*. Beirut: Dar al-Adab.
———. 2000. *al-Ghulama*. Beirut and London: Dar al-Saqi.
———. 2003. *al-Mahbubat*. Beirut and London: Dar al-Saqi.
Mina, Hanna. 1954. *al-Masabih al-Zurq*. n.p.
———. 1969. *al-Thalj Ya'ti min al-Nafidhah*. Beirut: Dar al-Adab.
———. 1973. *al-Shams fi Yawm Gha'im*. n.p.
———. 1975. *Baqaya Suwar*. Damascus: Wizarat al-Thaqafa wa-al-Irshad al-Qawmi.
———. 1977. *al-Mustanqa'*. Beirut: Dar al-Adab.
———. 1984. *al-Rabi'wa-al-Khareef*. Beirut: Dar al-Adab.
———. 2002. *Hamama Zarka' fi al-Suhub*. 4th ed. Beirut: Dar al-Adab.

al-Muhsin, Fatima. 2005. Review of *Makyaj Khafif li-Hadhih al-Layla. Al-Riyadh,* September 15. Accessed August 2009. http://www.alriyadh.com/2005/09/15/article94014.html.

al-Muji, Sahar. 1998. *Sayyidat al-Manam.* Cairo: Dar Sharqiyat.

Nuwaylati, Huyam. 1958. *al-Ghazali: Hayatuh,'Aqidatuh.* Damascus: al-Matba'a al-Jadida.

———. 1959. *Fi al-Layl.* Syria: n.p.

———. 1974a. *Kayfa Tumahhi al-Ab'ad.* Beirut: n.p.

———. 1974b. *Washm 'ala al-Hawa'.* Beirut: al-Ahlia li-al-Nashr wa-al-Tawzi'.

Qasim, Ziad. 1988a. *al-Mudir al-'Amm.* Aman: Wakalat al-Tawzi al-Urduniyya.

———. 1988b. *Abna' al-Qal'a.* 1st ed. n.p.

———. 1994–1996. *al-Zawba'a.* 2 vols. Aman: Matba'at al-Qabas: Manshurat Amanat.

———. 1998. *Abna' al-Qal'a.* 3d ed. Beirut: al-Mu'assasa al-'Arabiyya li-al-Dirasat wa-al-Nashr.

———. 2000. *al-Khasirun.* Beirut: al-Mu'assasa al-'Arabiyya li-al-Dirasat wa-al-Nashr. Dirasat wa-al-Nashr.

Rifa'iya, Yaseen. 2004. "al-Ghiwayah fi Hudn al-Mawt." *al-Mustaqbal,* January 14, 20.

al-Saadawi, Nawal. 1983. *Mudhakkirat Tabiba.* Cairo: Maktabat Madbuli.

———. 1986. "La Shaya' Yafna." In *Lahzat Siddq,* 77–82. Beirut: Dar al-Adab.

Sha'aban, Buthayna. 1999. *Mi'at 'Am min al-Riwaya al-Nisa'iya al-'Arabiyya.* Beirut: Dar al-Adab.

al-Sharqawi, 'Abd al-Rahman. 1954. *al-Ard.* Cairo: Dar al-Nashr.

al-Shaykh, Hanan. 1971. *Intihar Rajul Mayyit.* Beirut: Dar an-Nahar.

———. 1975. *Faras al-Shaytan.* Beirut: Dar an-Nahar.

———. 1980. *Hikayat Zahra.* Beirut: Hanan al-Shaykh.

———. 1982. *Wardat al-Sahra'.* Beirut: al-Mu'assasa al-Jami'iya li-al-Dirasat wa-al-Nashr.

———. 1988. *Misk al-Ghazal.* Beirut: Dar al-Adab.

———. 1994. *Aknusu al-Shams 'an al-Sutuh.* Beirut: Dar al-Adab.

———. 2001. *Innaha Landan ya 'Azizi.* Beirut: Dar al-Adab.

al-Siba'i, Yusuf. 1956. *al-Saqqa Mat.* Cairo: Dar Roz al-Yusuf.

———. 1969. *Nahnu la Nazra'u al-Shawk.* 2 vols. Cairo: Dar Misr li-al-Tiba'a.

al-Tahawy, Miral. 1995. *Reem al-Barari al-Mustahila.* Cairo: al-Haya al-Misriya al-'Amma li-al-Kitab.

———. 1996. *al-Khiba'*. Cairo: Dar Sharqiyat.

———. 1998. *al-Badhinjana al-Zarqa'*. Cairo: Dar Sharqiyat.

———. 2003. *Naqarat al-Ziba'*. Beirut: Dar al-Adab.

al-Takarli, Fuad. 1980. *al-Raj' al-Ba'id*. Beirut: Dar Ibn Rushd li-al-Tiba'a wa-al-Nashr.

Tarabishi, George. 1981. *Ramziyat al-Mar'a fi al-Riwaya al-'Arabiyya wa-Dirasat Ukhra*. Beirut: Dar al-Tali'a.

Taymur, Mahmoud. 1925. *'Amm Mutawalli*. Cairo: al-Matba'a al-Salafiya.

———. 1925–1926. *al-Shaykh Jum'a wa-Aqasis Ukhra*. 1st ed. n.p.

———. 1927. *al-Shaykh Jum'a wa-Aqasis Ukhra*. 2d ed. Cairo: al-Matba'a al-Salafiyya.

———. 1969. "Wa Usdila al Sitar." In *Ana al-Qatil wa-Qisas Ukhra*, 105–18. Cairo: Dar Nahdat Misr.

Telmissany, May. 1997. *Dunyazad*. Cairo: Dar Sharqiyat.

al-Wakil, Sa'id. 2004. *al-Jasad fi al-Riwaya al-'Arabiyya*. Cairo: al-Haya al-'Amma li-Qusur al-Thaqafa.

al-Zayyat, Latifa. 1960. *al-Bab al-Maftuh*. Cairo: Anglo Bookshop.

INDEX